Container & Prefab
HOUSE PLANS

monsa

Introduction

Container & Prefab House Plans contain more than 250 floor and elevation plans, as well as constructive details of 36 housing projects, both prefabricated and made with cargo containers.

Apart from containing all the necessary information and the guidelines that must be followed to build the project, they also help us to define the different spaces and their future furniture.

We all have in our minds an image of our ideal home. This book provides the tips and design ideas to make this dream come true, in addition to all the measures that will allow to organize and design the desired space, becoming an essential ally for the architect.

Container & Prefab House Plans contiene más de 250 planos de plantas, secciones y alzados, así como detalles constructivos de un total de 36 proyectos de viviendas, tanto prefabricadas como realizadas con contenedores de carga.

Los planos son fundamentales para guiar la obra, contienen toda la información necesaria y las pautas que se han de seguir para construir el proyecto, nos ayudarán a definir las áreas de la vivienda y también su futuro mobiliario.

Todos tenemos en la mente una imagen de nuestro hogar ideal. Este libro proporciona la fuente de consejos e ideas de diseño para hacer este sueño realidad, además de todas las medidas que permitirán organizar y diseñar el espacio deseado, convirtiéndose en un aliado esencial para el arquitecto.

CONTAINER

PREFAB

Shipping Container House

Studio H:T
Nederland (Colorado), USA
Photos © Braden Gumen
Number of Containers: 2

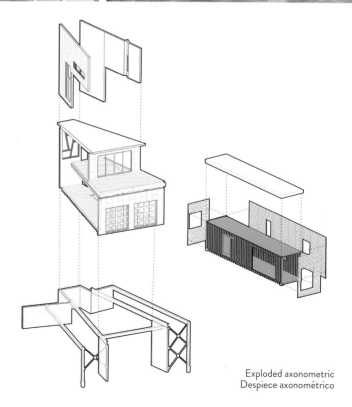
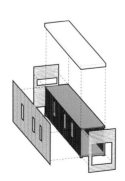

Exploded axonometric
Despiece axonométrico

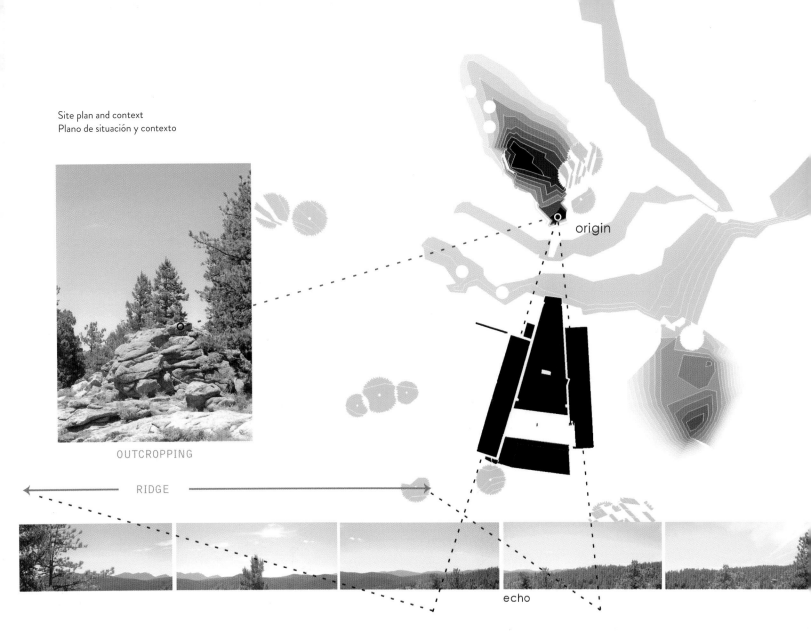

Site plan and context
Plano de situación y contexto

OUTCROPPING

RIDGE

origin

echo

A. Entry
B. Dining area
C. Living area
D. Bedroom
E. Bathroom
F. Office
G. Laundry / mechanical room
H. Kitchen
 I. Deck
J. Loft
K. Deck with pull-out bed
L. Green roof

A. Entrada
B. Zona de comedor
C. Zona de estar
D. Dormitorio
E. Baño
F. Despacho
G. Lavandería / sala de máquinas
H. Cocina
 I. Cubierta
J. Loft
K. Cubierta con sofá-cama
L. Tejado vegetal

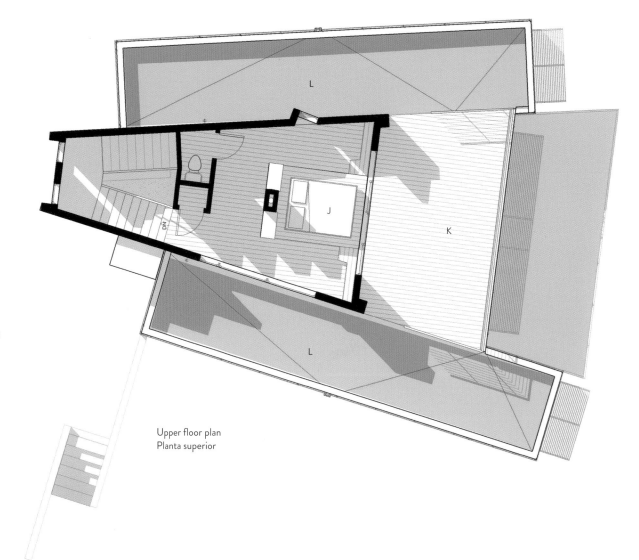

Upper floor plan
Planta superior

Lower floor plan
Planta inferior

WFH House

Arcgency
Wuxi, China
Photos © Jens Markus Lindhe, Mads Moller
Number of Containers: 2

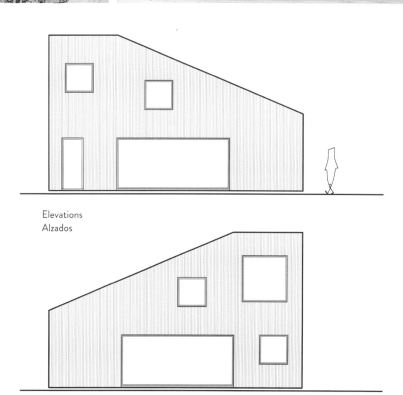

Elevations
Alzados

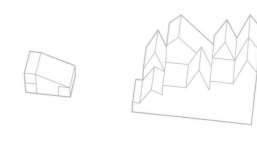

A. One family house.

B. Row house, Two family house.

C. Two, three family house.

D. Small one family house.

E. Town houses. From 1 to 6 stories high.

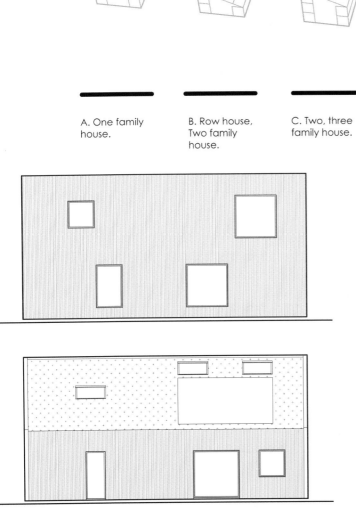

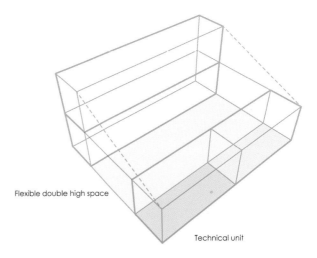

Flexible double high space

Technical unit

- Solar Cells, 30 m² (Roof facing south)
- Green Roof
- Rainwater is collected in underground storage
- Sky lights

- Highly insulated wall. 350 mm
- Bamboo façade (Interchangeable façade system)
- Windows that facilitates differentiated light

- Containers or flexible steel frame system (can be transported as regular ISO containers)
- Top class indoor climate
- Durable, healthy materials.

- Heat pump
- Water tank
- Possible to connect to ground heating
- Energy management system, online tracking of energy consumption / production

- Paving that absorbers storm water
- Large opening to the surroundings / nature

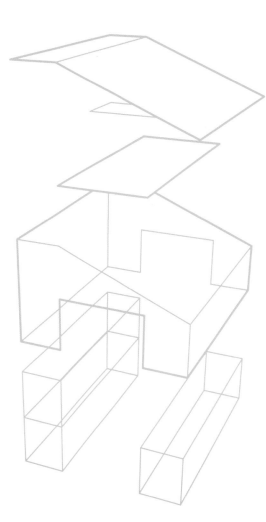

- Celdas solares, 30 m² (Tejado orientado al sur)
- Techo ecológico
- El agua de lluvia se recoge en el depósito subterráneo.
- Luces *Sky*

- Gran aislamiento de la pared. 350 mm
- Fachada de bambú (Sistema de fachada intercambiable)
- Windows que facilita la refractación de la luz.

- Contenedores o sistema de marco de acero flexible (puede ser transportado como contenedores estándar ISO)
- Alta eficiencia climática interior.
- Materiales duraderos y saludables.

- Bomba de calor.
- Tanque de agua.
- Opción de conexión de la calefacción en el suelo.
- Sistema de gestión de energía, seguimiento en línea del consumo y producción de energía.

- El pavimento absorve el agua de la lluvia.
- Gran apertura al entorno / naturaleza.

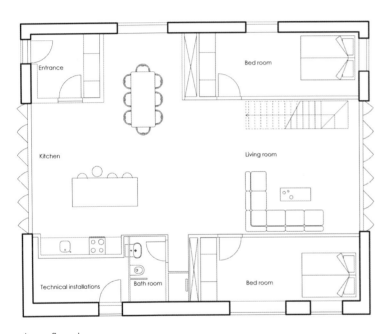

Entrance

Bed room

Kitchen

Living room

Technical installations

Bath room

Bed room

Lower floor plan
Planta inferior

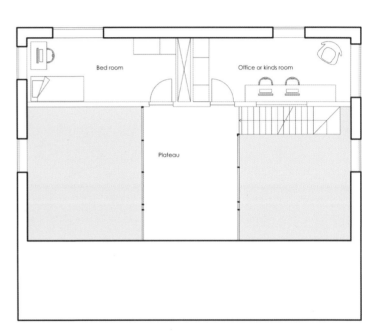

Bed room

Office or kinds room

Plateau

Upper floor plan
Planta superior

Six Oaks

Modulus
Felton (California), USA
Photos © Modulus
Number of Containers: 6

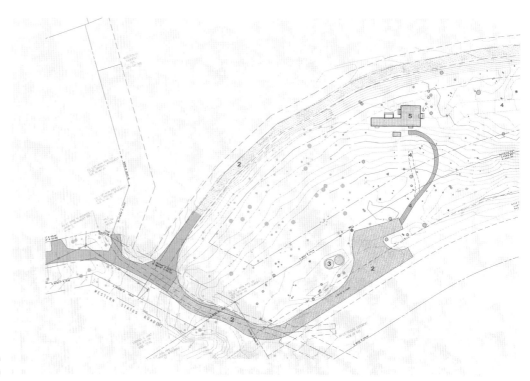

Sitemap plan
Plano de localización

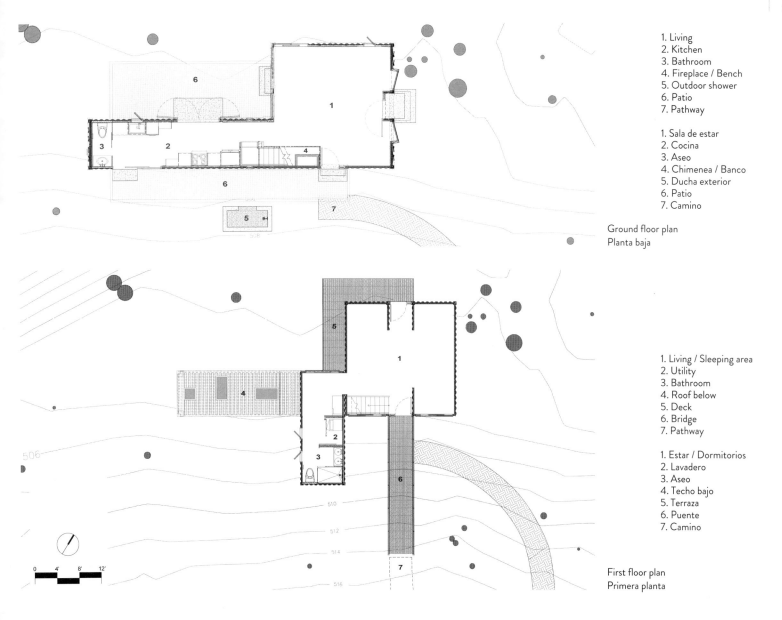

1. Living
2. Kitchen
3. Bathroom
4. Fireplace / Bench
5. Outdoor shower
6. Patio
7. Pathway

1. Sala de estar
2. Cocina
3. Aseo
4. Chimenea / Banco
5. Ducha exterior
6. Patio
7. Camino

Ground floor plan
Planta baja

1. Living / Sleeping area
2. Utility
3. Bathroom
4. Roof below
5. Deck
6. Bridge
7. Pathway

1. Estar / Dormitorios
2. Lavadero
3. Aseo
4. Techo bajo
5. Terraza
6. Puente
7. Camino

First floor plan
Primera planta

0   4'   8'   12'

Conceptual parameters and initiatives:
1. Recycled shipping containers
2. Insulated foam cool roof
3. Pier foundation allows water to filter naturally minimizing grading
4. Raised foundation creates shower and outdoor space
5. Centrally located fireplace for warmth and home
6. Skylights collect and filter natural daylight
7. Natural ventilation & operable hight efficiency windows/doors
8. Two total trees removed and recycled into interior components
9. Existing container floors refinished and reused
10. Interior bridge connects to canopy level
11. Metal grate bridge connects home to hillside

Parámetros e iniciativas conceptuales:
1. Contenedores de transporte reciclados
2. Espuma aislante para el tejado
3. El pozo de cimentación permite que el agua se filtre de manera natural minimizando la nivelación
4. Una base elevada permite crear una ducha y un espacio exterior
5. Chimenea ubicada en el centro para calentar la casa
6. Los tragaluces captan y filtran la luz del día natural
7. Ventilación natural y puertas/ventanas graduables de gran eficacia
8. Dos árboles talados y reciclados para los componentes del interior
9. El suelo de los contenedores se ha reutilizado y se le ha dado un acabado
10. La pasarela interior conecta con el nivel de las copas de los árboles
11. La pasarela de rejilla metálica conecta la casa con la ladera

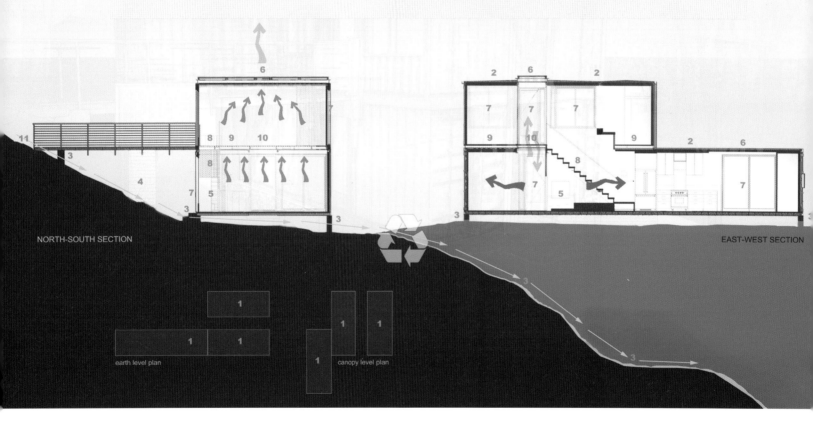

NORTH-SOUTH SECTION

EAST-WEST SECTION

earth level plan

canopy level plan

Heating, cooling, and sun response:
1. Centrally located Fireplace
2. Natural ventilation & operable windows/skylights
3. Closed cell insulation
4. Site selection and building orientation
5. Large skylight spine to collect and filter daylight
6. Metal grate bridge filters light to ower level

Materials, Site and Sustainability:
1. Recycled shipping containers
2. Insulated foam cool roof
3. Two total trees removed and recycled into interior components
4. Existing container flor refinished and reused
5. Low-E High efficiency windows
6. Pier foundation allows water to filter naturally minimizing grading

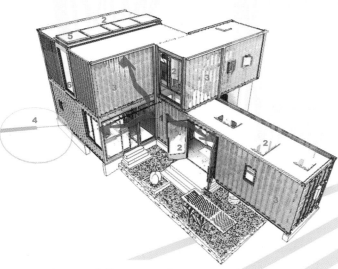

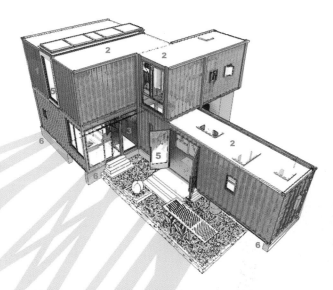

Calefacción, ventilación y respuesta solar:
1. Chimenea ubicada en el centro
2. Ventilación natural y tragaluces/ventanas graduables
3. Aislamiento de célula cerrada
4. Elección del emplazamiento y orientación del edificio
5. Gran columna de tragaluz para captar y filtrar la luz del sol
6. La pasarela de rejilla metálica filtra la luz hasta los niveles más bajos

Materiales, emplazamiento y sostenibilidad:
1. Contenedores de transporte reciclados
2. Espuma aislante para el tejado
3. Dos árboles talados y reciclados para los componentes del interior
4. El suelo de los contenedores se ha reutilizado y se le ha dado un acabado
5. Ventanas de gran eficiencia y baja emisión
6. El pozo de cimentación permite que el agua se filtre de manera natural minimizando la nivelación

Two-Family House

Oskar Leo Kaufman and Bmst Johannes Kaufmann
Andelsbuch, Austria
Photos © Ignacio Martínez

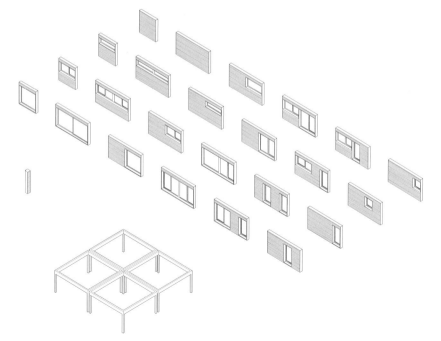

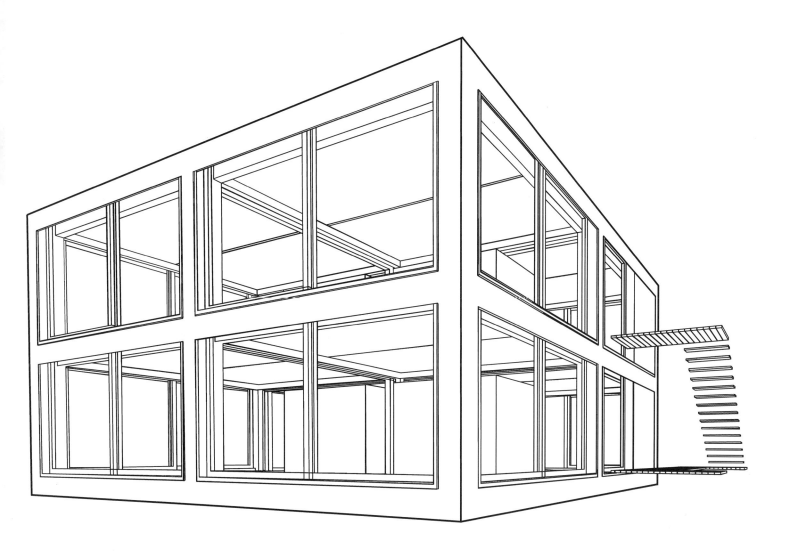

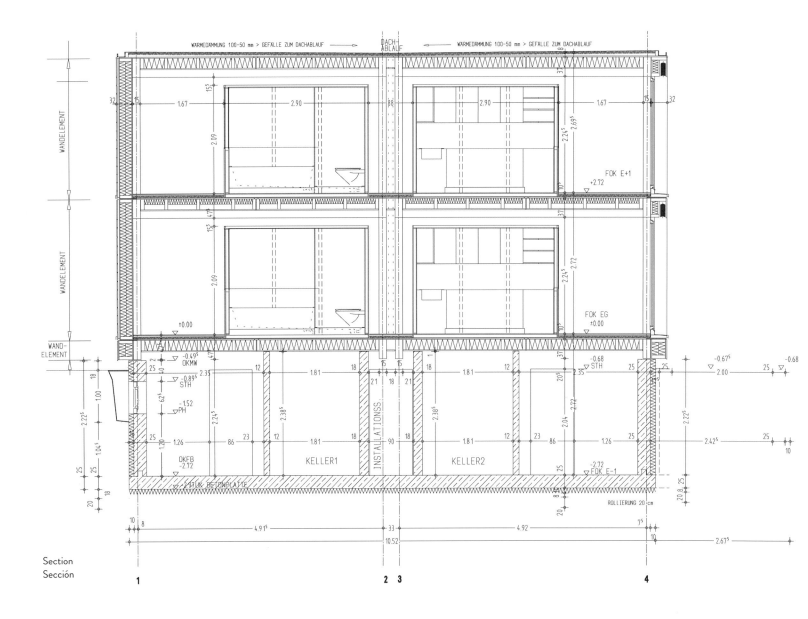

WÄRMEDÄMMUNG 100-50 mm > GEFÄLLE ZUM DACHABLAUF →   DACH-ABLAUF   ← WÄRMEDÄMMUNG 100-50 mm > GEFÄLLE ZUM DACHABLAUF

WANDELEMENT

WANDELEMENT

WAND-ELEMENT

FOK E+1
+2.72

FOK EG
+0.00

±0.00

OKMW
STH
PH
OKFB

KELLER1

INSTALLATIONSS.

KELLER2

STH

FOK E-1

STAHLK.BETONPLATTE

ROLLIERUNG 20 cm

Section
Sección

1   2 3   4

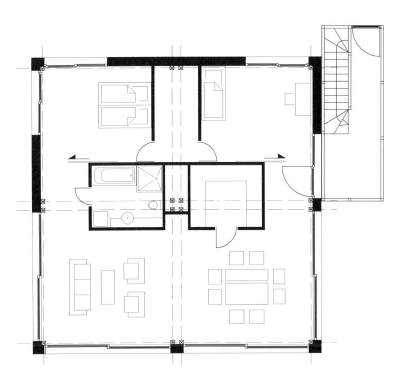

Main plan floor
Planta piso principal

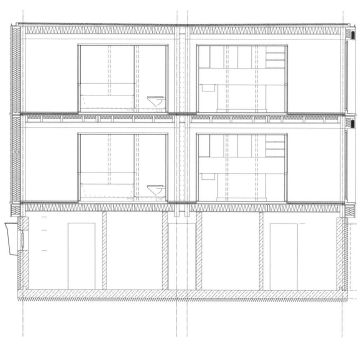

Section
Sección

Un Dernier Voyage

Spray architecture & Gabrielle Vella-Boucaud
Meuse, France
Photos © Jelena Stajic
Area: 110 m²

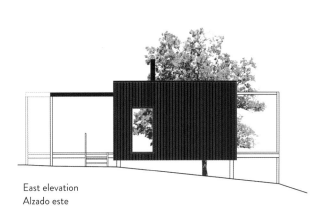

East elevation
Alzado este

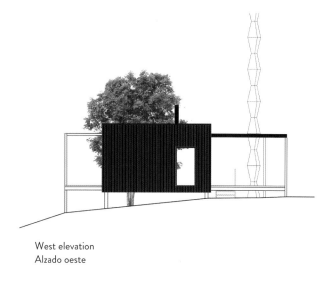

West elevation
Alzado oeste

North elevation
Alzado norte

South elevation
Alzado sur

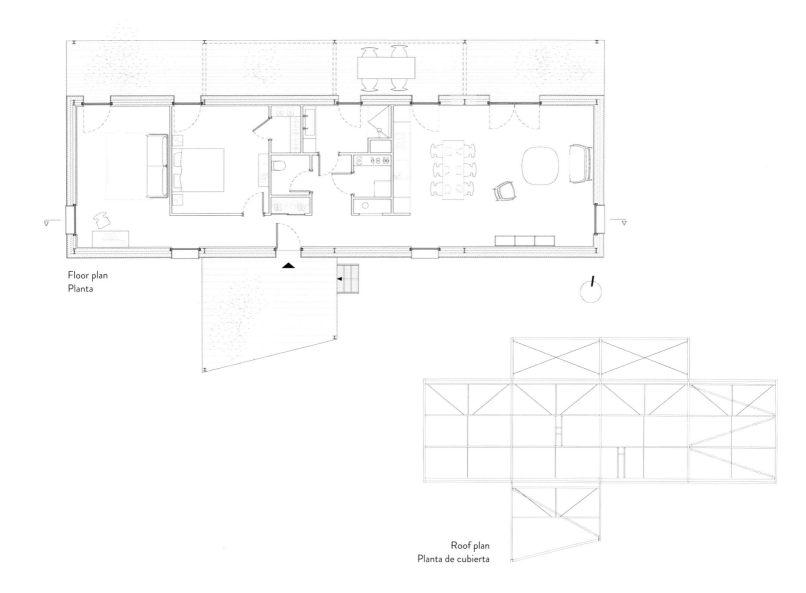

Floor plan
Planta

Roof plan
Planta de cubierta

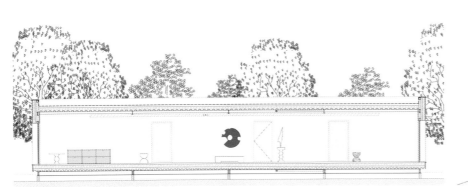

Longitudinal section
Sección longitudinal

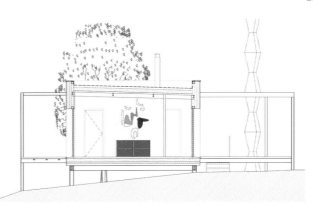

Cross section
Sección transversal

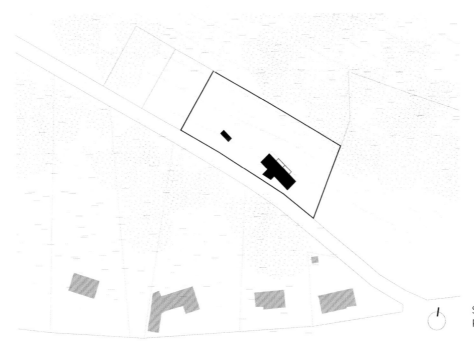

Sitemap plan
Plano de localización

Casa Mía

Matias Pons Estel
Santo Tomé (Santa Fe), Argentina
Photos © Federico Cairoli
Area: 36 m²

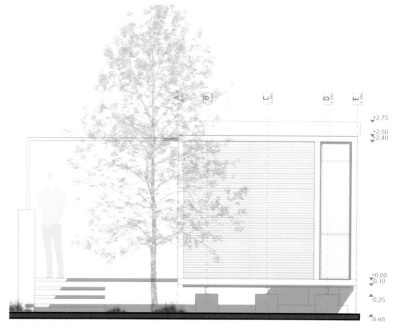

West elevation
Alzado oeste

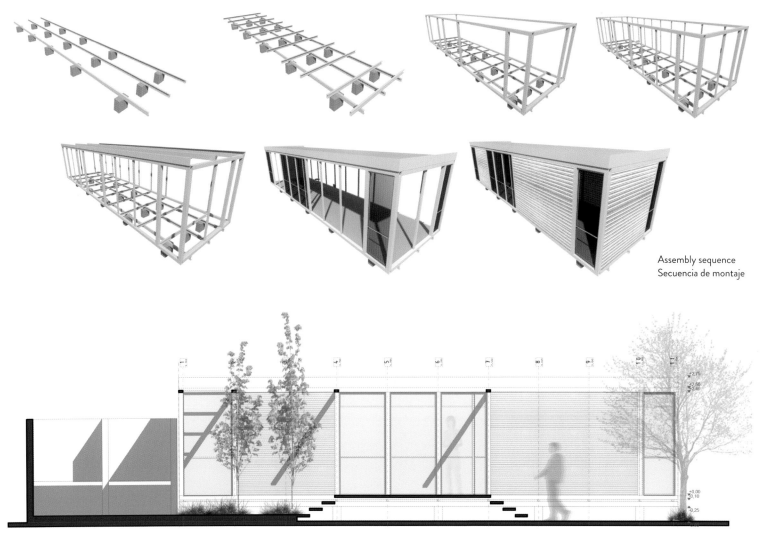

Assembly sequence
Secuencia de montaje

North elevation
Alzado norte

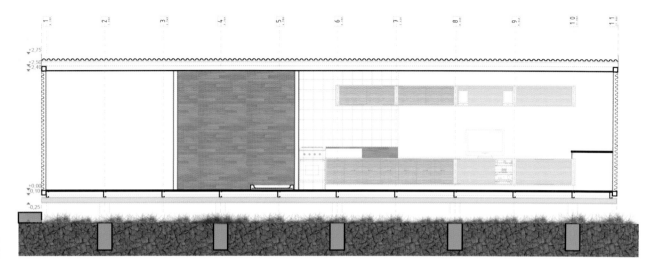

Longitudinal section
Sección longitudinal

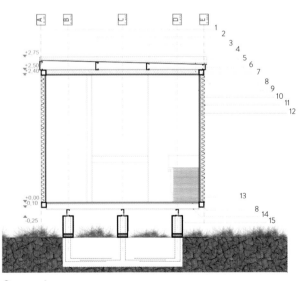

Cross section
Sección transversal

1. Galvanized steel angle C 160
2. Galvanized steel angle C 140
3. Galvanized steel angle C 120
4. Galvanized steel angle C 100
5. Galvanized sheet #20
6. Rockwool insulation
7. Gypboard ceiling
8. Perimeter tube 100 x 100 x 2 mm
9. Gypboard wall
10. Extruded polystyrene
11. Galvanized sheet GA 20
12. Galvanized steel angle C 80 x 50 x 20 x 2 mm
13. OSB 18 mm, asphalt paint finish
14. Galvanized steel angle C 120 x 50 x 20 x 2 mm
15. Galvanized steel angle C 120 attached to foundation piers

1. Ángulo de acero galvanizado C 160
2. Ángulo de acero galvanizado C 140
3. Ángulo de acero galvanizado C 120
4. Ángulo de acero galvanizado C 100
5. Hoja galvanizada #20
6. Aislamiento Rockwool
7. Techo pladur
8. Tubo de perímetro 100 x 100 x 2 mm
9. Pared Pladur
10. Poliestireno expandido
11. Hoja galvanizada GA 20
12. Ángulo de acero galvanizado C 80 x 50 x 20 x 2 mm
13. OSB 18 mm, acabado de pintura asfáltica
14. Ángulo de acero galvanizado C 120 x 50 x 20 x 2 mm
15. Ángulo de acero galvanizado C 120 sujeto a los cimientos

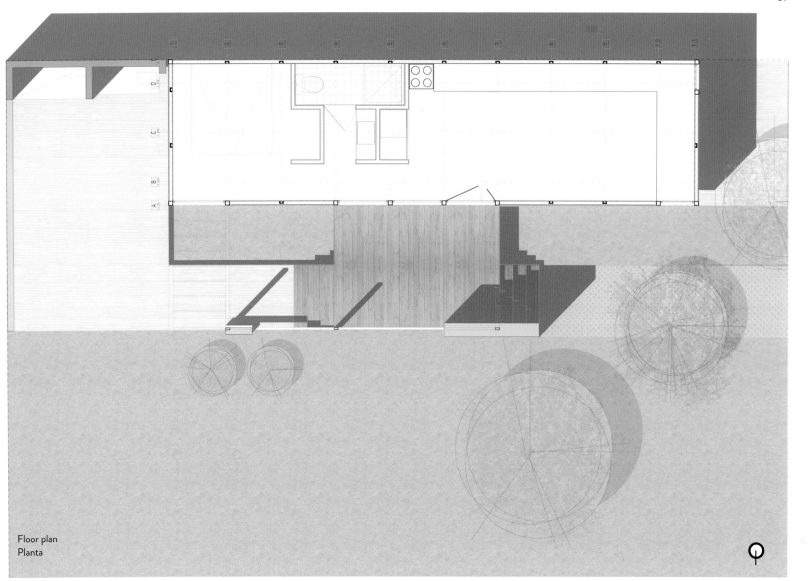

Floor plan
Planta

Red Containers House

Patrick Partouche Architecte
Lille, France
Photos © Patrick Partouche
Number of Containers: 8

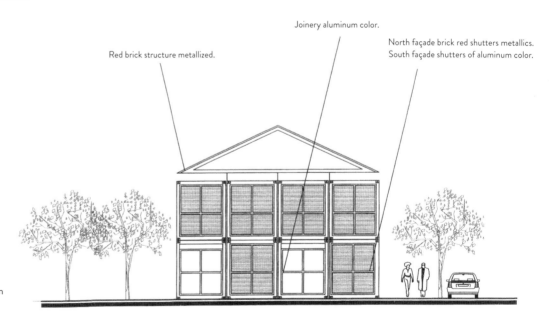

Joinery aluminum color.

Red brick structure metallized.

North façade brick red shutters metallics.
South façade shutters of aluminum color.

South elevation
Alzado sur

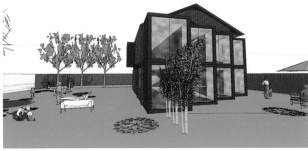

Red brick structure metallized.
Estructura de ladrillo rojo metalizado.

Roof as a checkerboard made with 50% Terracota
red color tile shingles and 50% empty.
Cubierta a modo de damero compuesto por un
50% de tejas rojas de terracota y el 50% vacía.

Joinery aluminum color.
Carpintería de color aluminio.

North façade brick red shutters metallics.
South façade shutters of aluminum color.
Fachada norte de ladrillo rojo con postigos.
Fachada sur con persianas de color aluminio.

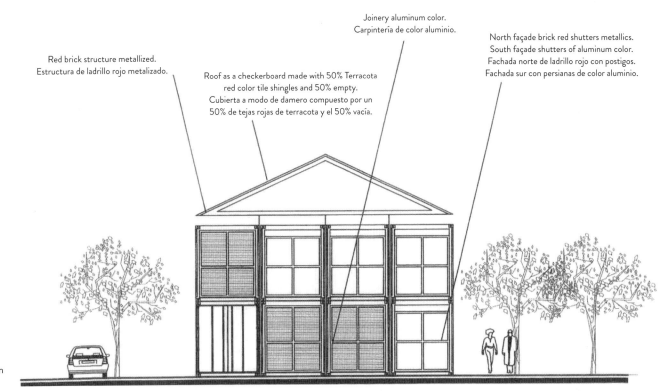

North elevation
Alzado norte

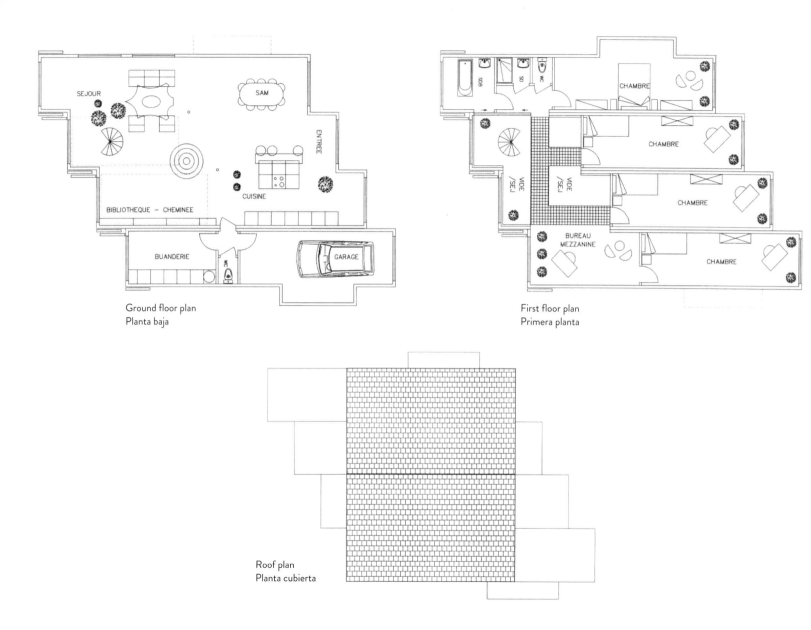

Ground floor plan
Planta baja

First floor plan
Primera planta

Roof plan
Planta cubierta

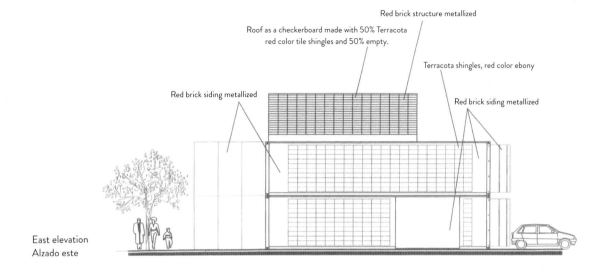

Red brick structure metallized

Roof as a checkerboard made with 50% Terracota red color tile shingles and 50% empty.

Terracota shingles, red color ebony

Red brick siding metallized

Red brick siding metallized

East elevation
Alzado este

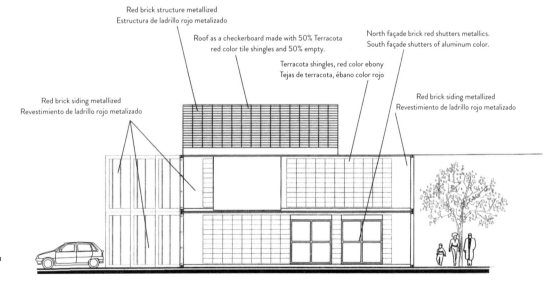

Red brick structure metallized
Estructura de ladrillo rojo metalizado

Roof as a checkerboard made with 50% Terracota red color tile shingles and 50% empty.

North façade brick red shutters metallics.
South façade shutters of aluminum color.

Terracota shingles, red color ebony
Tejas de terracota, ébano color rojo

Red brick siding metallized
Revestimiento de ladrillo rojo metalizado

Red brick siding metallized
Revestimiento de ladrillo rojo metalizado

West elevation
Alzado oeste

Zigloo Domestique

Keith Dewey
Victoria area, Canada
Photos © Nik West
Number of Containers: 9

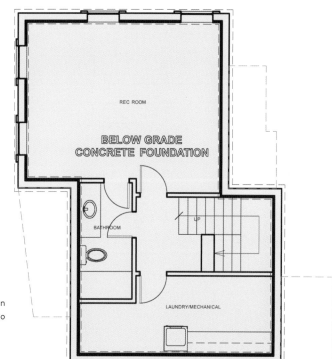

REC ROOM

**BELOW GRADE
CONCRETE FOUNDATION**

BATHROOM

UP

LAUNDRY/MECHANICAL

Lower floor plan
Planta sótano

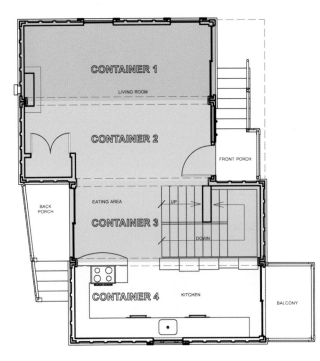

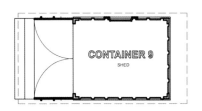

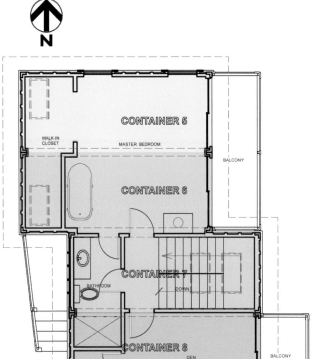

Level 2 floor plan
Planta segunda

Level 3 floor plan
Planta tercera

The Crib

Broadhurst Architects
Bethesda (Maryland), USA
Photos © Anice Hoachlander

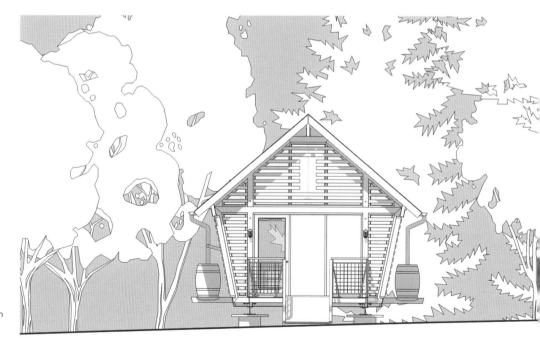

Front elevation
Alzado frontal

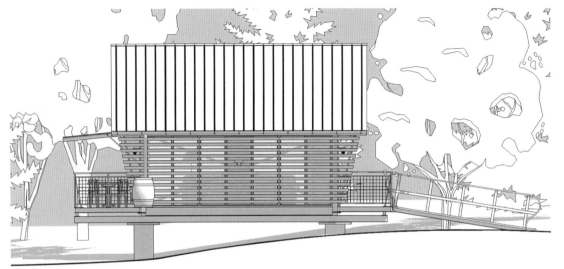

Side elevation
Alzado lateral

Rear elevation
Alzado posterior

1. Foundation
1. Cimientos

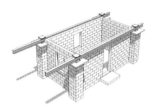

2. Install steel beams
2. Instalación vigas acero

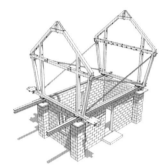

3. Install steel bents and braces
3. Instalación de soportes en acero doblado

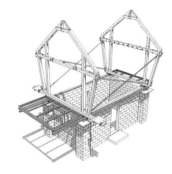

4. Install steel deck frames
4. Instalación de estructuras de acero del suelo

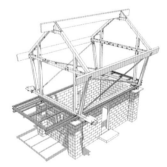

5. Install parallam beams
5. Instalación vigas parallam

6. Install structural insulated panels
6. Instalación de paneles aislantes estructurales

7. Install wood and polycarbonate panels
7. Instalación de paneles de madera y policarbonato

8. Install fiberglass deck, metal rails, awning, rain barrels and roof
8. Instalación de suelo de fibra de vidrio, rieles metálicos, toldos, barriles de agua de lluvia y techo

Assembly sequence
Secuencia de montaje

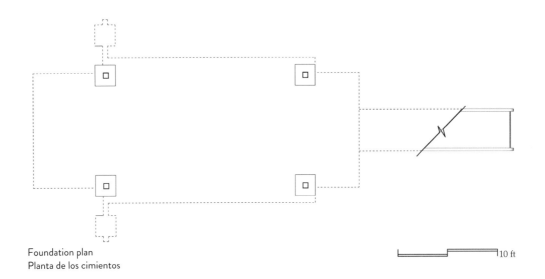

Foundation plan
Planta de los cimientos

10 ft

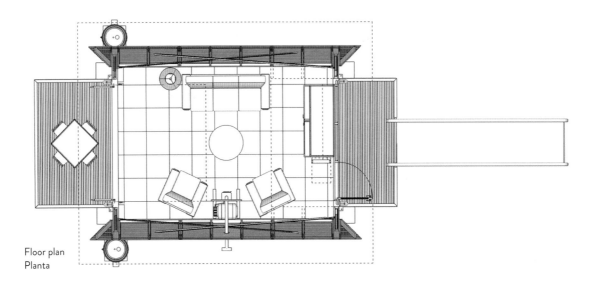

Floor plan
Planta

Refugio en Huentelauquen

Pablo Errázuriz
Huentelauquen (IV Región), Chile
Photos © Pablo Errázuriz
Number of Containers: 1

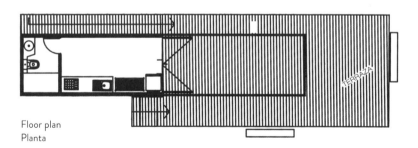

Floor plan
Planta

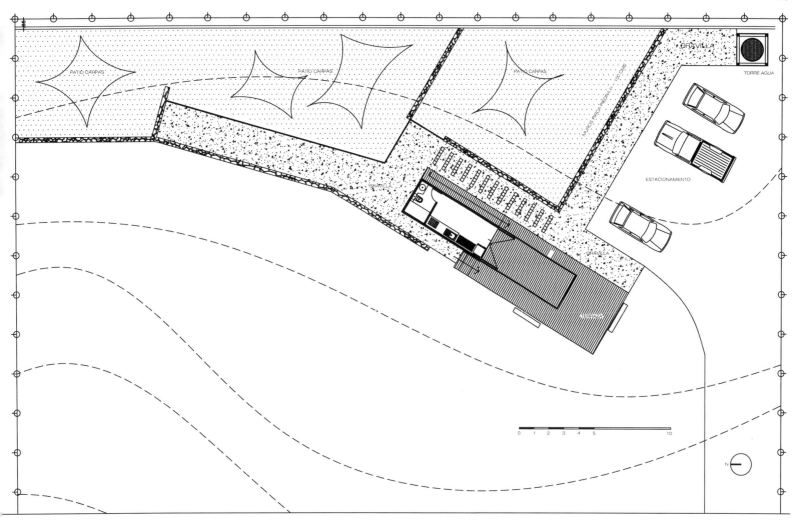

PATIO CARPAS

PATIO CARPAS

PATIO CARPAS

GRAVILLA

TORRE AGUA

ESTACIONAMIENTO

GRAVILLA

GRAVILLA

0 1 2 3 4 5   10

N

Site plan
Plano de situación

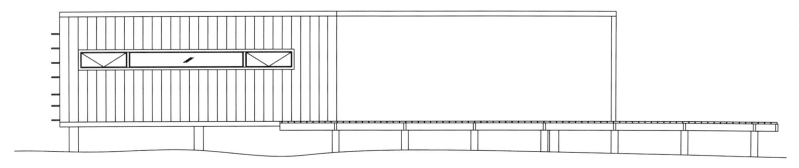

West elevation
Alzado oeste

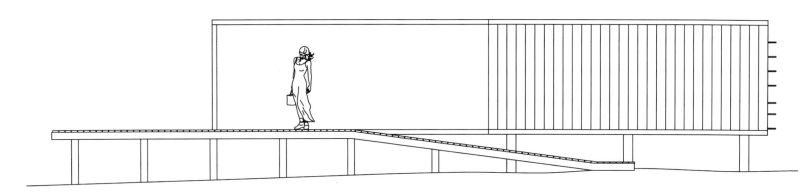

East elevation
Alzado este

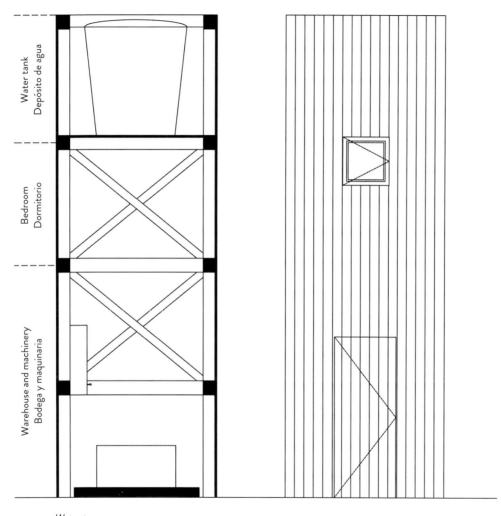

Water tank
Depósito de agua

Bedroom
Dormitorio

Warehouse and machinery
Bodega y maquinaria

Water tower
Torre de agua

Predominant materials:

- 20 feet container
- Stone walls
- Gravel
- Wood (impregnated pine)
- Sand

Materiales predominantes:

- Container de 20 pies
- Muros de piedra
- Gravilla
- Madera (pino impregnado)
- Arena

0   0.5   1.0   1.5   2.0   2.5

Modular 4

Studio 804
Kansas City (Kansas), USA
Photos © Studio 804
Modules: 7

Site plan
Plano de situación

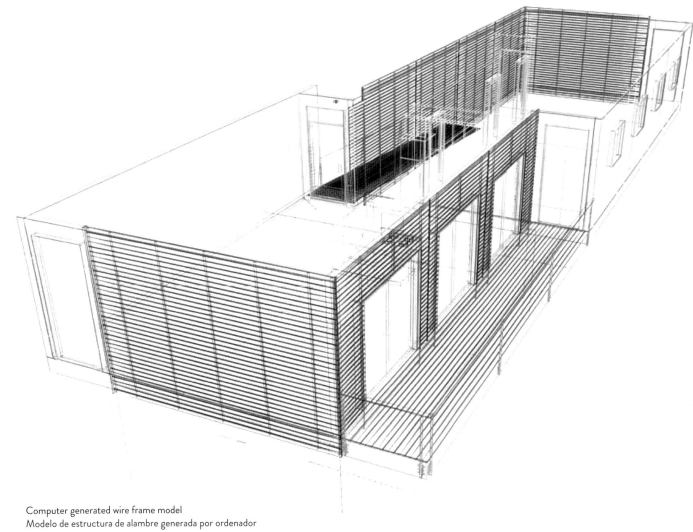

Computer generated wire frame model
Modelo de estructura de alambre generada por ordenador

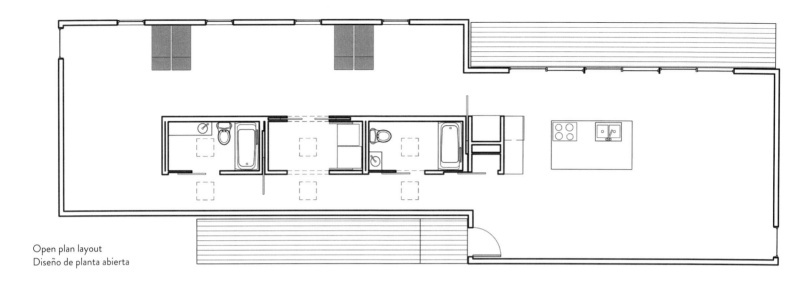

Open plan layout
Diseño de planta abierta

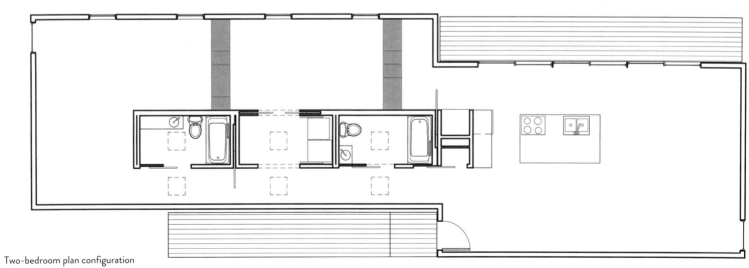

Two-bedroom plan configuration
Configuración de planta con 2 dormitorios

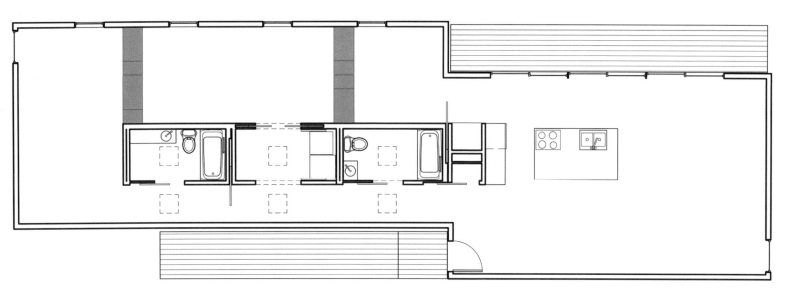

Three-bedroom plan configuration
Configuración de planta con 3 dormitorios

Container Guest House

Poteet Architects
San Antonio (Texas), USA
Photos © Chris Cooper

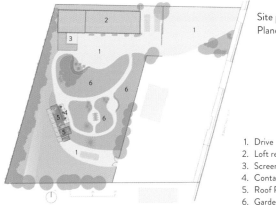

Site plan
Plano de situación

1. Drive
2. Loft residence
3. Screened entry
4. Container
5. Roof Planters
6. Garden

1. Camino
2. Residencia
3. Entrada acristalada
4. Container
5. Techo con plantas
6. Jardín

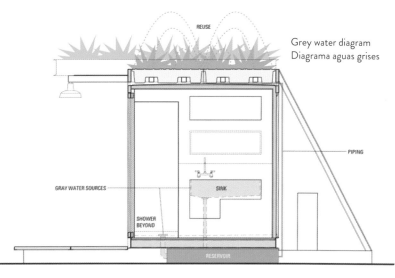

Grey water diagram
Diagrama aguas grises

1. Gray water sources
2. Shower beyond
3. Sink
4. Reservoir
5. Piping
6. Reuse

1. Salida aguas grises
2. Ducha
3. Lavamanos
4. Depósito
5. Tubería
6. Reutilización

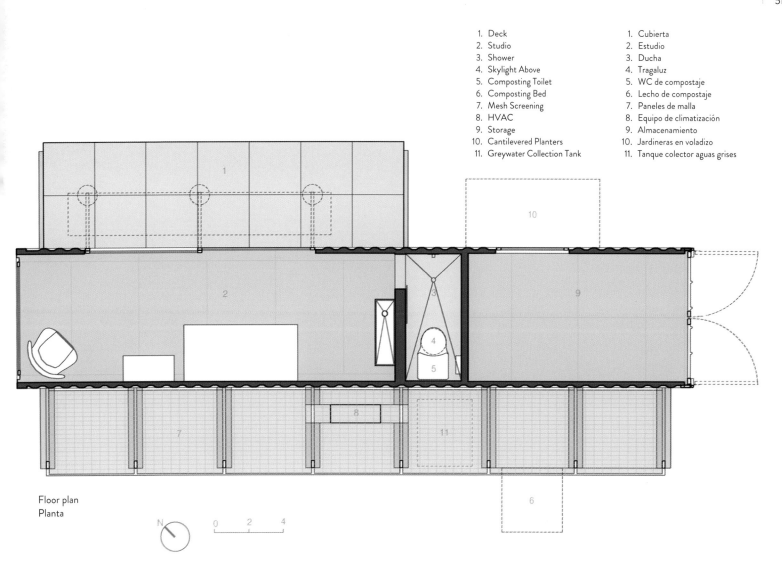

1. Deck
2. Studio
3. Shower
4. Skylight Above
5. Composting Toilet
6. Composting Bed
7. Mesh Screening
8. HVAC
9. Storage
10. Cantilevered Planters
11. Greywater Collection Tank

1. Cubierta
2. Estudio
3. Ducha
4. Tragaluz
5. WC de compostaje
6. Lecho de compostaje
7. Paneles de malla
8. Equipo de climatización
9. Almacenamiento
10. Jardineras en voladizo
11. Tanque colector aguas grises

Floor plan
Planta

N   0   2   4

Artist Studio

Open Studio Pty Ltd
Flemington (Melbourne), Australia
Photos © Open Studio

Detail Door Head D01 @ 1:5

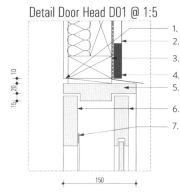

15 | 20 | 10

150

Detail Door Sill D01 @ 1:5

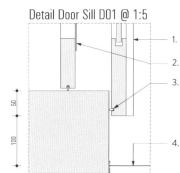

50

100

DETAIL DOOR HEAD D01

1. Casing bead.
2. Wall cladding.
3. Folded metal flashing 150 mm min. upstand.
4. Profiled closed cell infill.
5. Timber door head clear finish.
6. Timber door head clear finish.
7. Flyscreen stapled to timber frame.

DETALLE SUPERIOR PUERTA D01

1. Junta.
2. Panel de fachada.
3. Tapajuntas de metal doblado 150 mm. mínimo.
4. Perfil de celda cerrada con relleno.
5. Puerta de madera acabada en claro.
6. Puerta de madera acabada en claro.
7. Mosquitera sujeta al marco de madera.

DETAIL DOOR SILL D01

1. Line of jamb.
2. Flyscreen stapled to timber frame.
3. Raven door seal.
4. Finished ground level.

DETALLE DE PUERTA UMBRAL D01

1. Línea de marco.
2. Mosquitera sujeta al marco de madera.
3. Junta flexible de puerta Raven.
4. Nivel de suelo.

Detail Door Jamb D01 @ 1:5

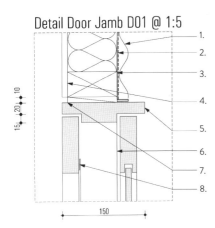

DETAIL DOOR JAMB D01
1. Wall cladding.
2. Vapour permeable sarking.
3. Folded metal flashing 150 mm min. aprox.
4. Silicon seal bottom plates 150 mm min. around all doors.
5. Timber door frame clear finish.
6. Edge of concrete slab.
7. Casing bead.
8. Flyscreen stapled to timber frame.

DETALLE LATERAL PUERTA MARCO D01
1. Panel de fachada.
2. Barrera de vapor.
3. Tapajuntas de metal doblado 150 mm. mínimo.
4. Sellado de silicona en pletinas inferiores mínimo 150 mm. alrededor de todas las puertas.
5. Puerta de madera acabada en claro.
6. Borde de la losa de hormigón.
7. Junta de cubierta.
8. Mosquitera con grapas a la madera marco.

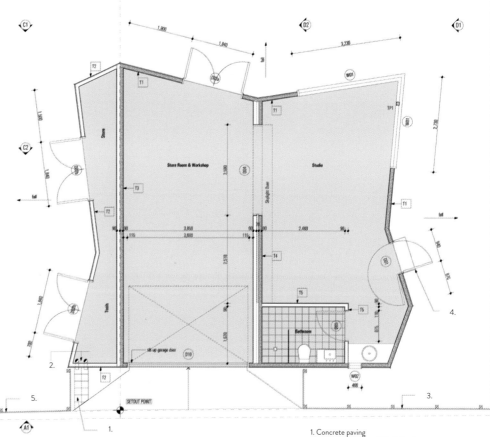

Main floor plan
Planta general

1. Concrete paving
2. Downpipes 100mm DIA (x2) min
3. New paling fence
4. Concrete steps
5. New paling fence

1. Baldosas de hormigón
2. Bajantes 100mm DIA (x2) min
3. Nueva valla
4. Escalones de hormigón
5. Nueva valla

ROOF

Metal roof deck, Klip-Lok 406 Zincalume finish.
Reflective foil laminate.
Timber structure RJ3 & RJ3.
Polyester insualtion R3.0 minimum.
Ceiling bettens.
Plasteboard 13mm THK, paint finish.

CUBIERTA

Cubierta de techo de metal, Klip-Lok 406 acabado Zincalume.
Reflectante de aluminio laminado.
Estructura de madera RJ3 & RJ3.
Aislante de poliéster R3.0 mínimo.
Listones de madera.
Placa de cartón yeso de13mm THK, acabada en pintura.

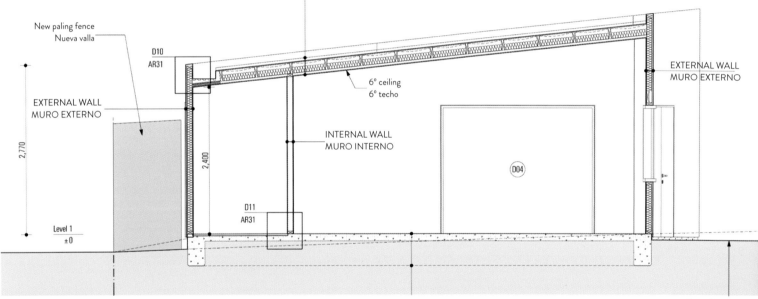

New paling fence
Nueva valla

D10
AR31

EXTERNAL WALL
MURO EXTERNO

EXTERNAL WALL
MURO EXTERNO

6° ceiling
6° techo

2,770

2,400

INTERNAL WALL
MURO INTERNO

D04

D11
AR31

Level 1
±0

Ground level.
Nivel del terreno.

Section D2 @ 1:50
Sección D2 @ 1:50

FLOOR

Floor finish.
Reinforced concrete slab as per structural drawings.
Moisture barrier polythene membrane.
Sand bed.

SUELO

Tratamiento de superficie.
Losa de hormigón armado según planos estructurales.
Membrana antihumedad de polietileno.
Base de arena.

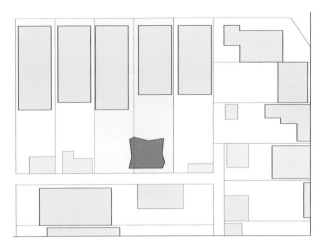

The new building is located in the shared space of the two shaded plots.
En las dos parcelas sombreadas y compartidas se ubica la nueva construcción.

Approx existing ground line.
Línea aproximada previa del terreno.

Detail D01 @ 1:10

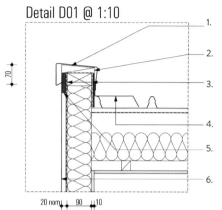

DETAIL D01

1. Folded pressed metal capping Colorbond finish.
2. Hardwood support screw fixed to framing.
3. Vapour permeable sarking.
4. Flashing overlap 2/3 pan width min.
5. Profiled closed-cell infill.
6. Wall cladding.

DETALLE D01

1. Remate metálico plegado con acabado Colorbond.
2. Bloque de madera fijado al entramado.
3. Barrera de vapor.
4. Panel solapado a dos tercios.
5. Perfil de celda cerrada con relleno.
6. Panel de fachada.

Detail D02 @ 1:10

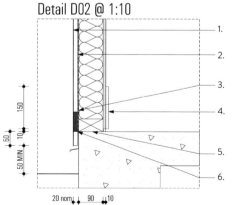

DETAIL D02

1. Wall cladding.
2. Vapour permeable sarking.
3. Metal flashing sealed to edge of slab, 150 mm MIN up-stand.
4. Skirting MDF, 10mm THK, painted finish.
5. Treated timber bottom plate on damp-proof course.
6. Profiled closed cell infill.

DETALLE D02

1. Panel de fachada.
2. Barrera de vapor.
3. Tapajuntas de metal sellado hasta el borde de la losa, 150 mm.
4. Zócalo de MDF, 10 mm THK pintado.
5. Pletina inferior de madera hidrófuga tratada.
6. Perfil de celda cerrada con relleno.

Nomad Living

studio arte
Algarve, Portugal
Photos © studio arte

Section 1
Sección 1

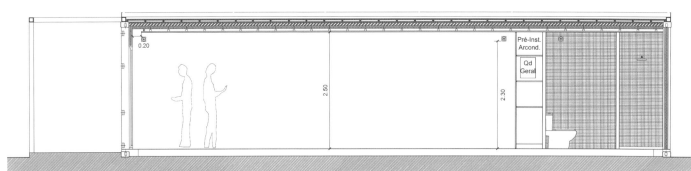

0.20

2.50

2.30

Pré-Inst.
Arcond.

Qd
Geral

0.40

Front elevation
Alzado frontal

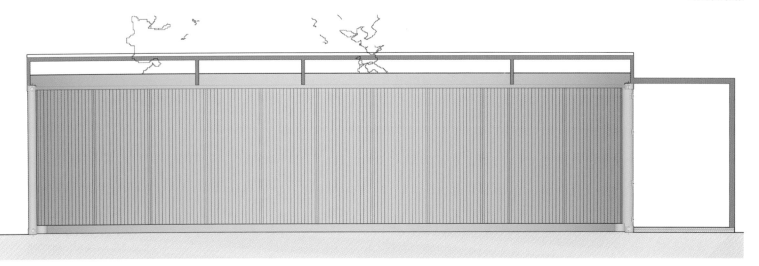

Back elevation
Alzado posterior

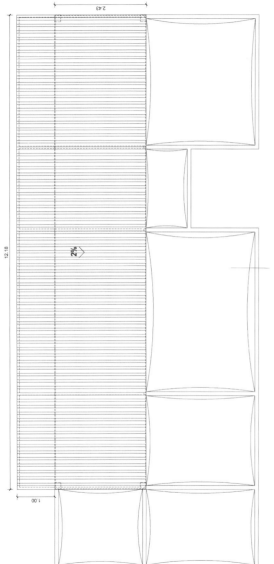

Roof plan
Planta cubierta

Right side elevation
Alzado lateral derecho

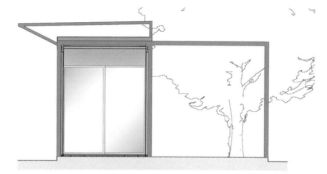

Left side elevation (doors open)
Alzado lateral izquierdo (puertas abiertas)

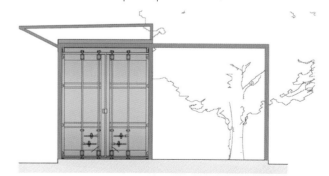

Left side elevation (doors closed)
Alzado lateral izquierdo (puertas cerradas)

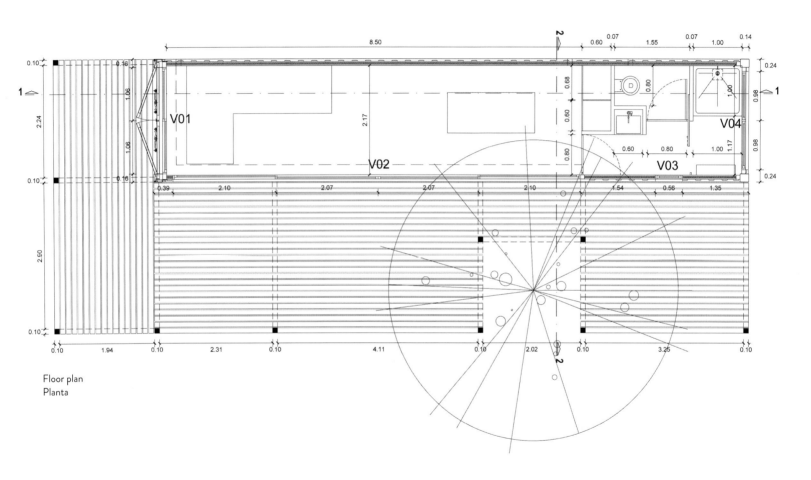

Floor plan
Planta

B-Line Medium 010

Hive Modular
Calgary (Alberta), Canada
Photos © Hive Modular
Modules: 2

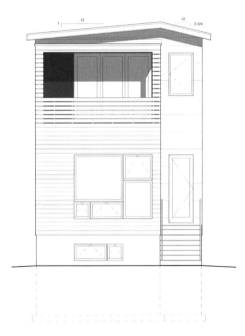

North elevation
Alzado norte

South elevation
Alzado sur

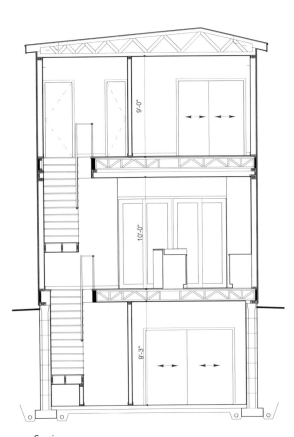

Section
Sección

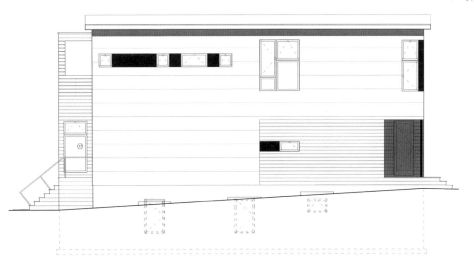

East elevation
Alzado este

West elevation
Alzado oeste

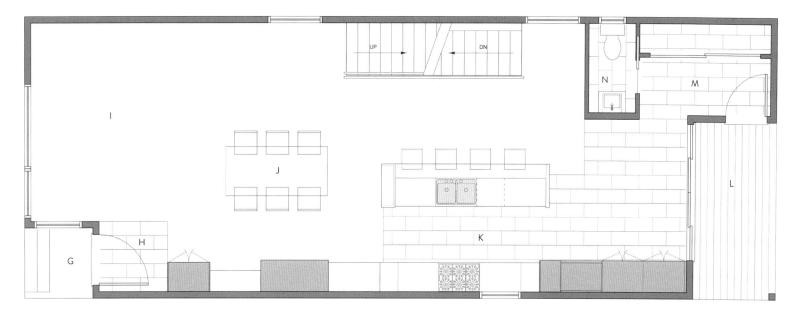

Main floor plan
Planta principal

A. Family room	J. Dining area	A. Sala de estar	J. Comedor
B. Bedroom	K. Kitchen	B. Dormitorio	K. Cocina
C. Storage	L. Covered deck	C. Almacenamiento	L. Terraza cubierta
D. Bathroom	M. Mud room	D. Baño	M. Vestíbulo
E. Laundry room	N. Powder room	E. Lavandería	N. Aseo
F. Mechanical room	O. Master bedroom	F. Cuarto de maquinaria	O. Dormitorio principal
G. Entry porch	P. Master bathroom	G. Porche de entrada	P. Baño principal
H. Entry foyer	Q. Linen closet	H. Entrada	Q. Vestidor
I. Living area	R. Open to below	I. Salón	R. Piso superior abierto con vista abajo

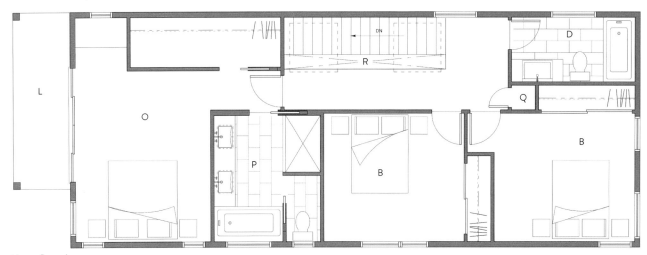

Upper floor plan
Planta superior

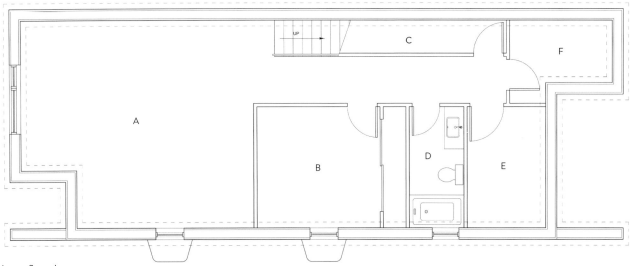

Lower floor plan
Planta inferior

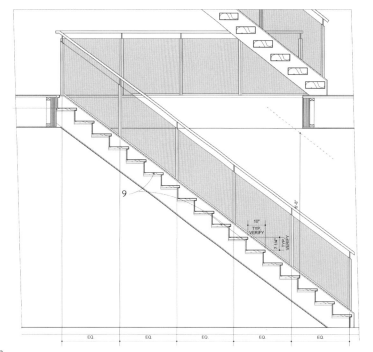

1. Hardwood handrail
2. Painted steel
3. Hardwood jamb and stop
4. Tempered clear glass
5. Hardwood tread and riser
6. Hardwood cap
7. 1/2" gypboard
8. Stringers
9. Assumes typical 3/4" finished
   hardwood tread

1. Pasamanos de madera
2. Acero pintado
3. Quicio y tope de puerta de madera
4. Vidrio templado transparente
5. Huella y contrahuella de los
   escalones, de madera
6. Acabado del suelo
7. Pladur 1/2"
8. Zancas
9. Acabado escalones de madera de 3/4"

Stair section. Inside, basement to main floor
Sección de escalera. Dentro, del sótano a la planta principal

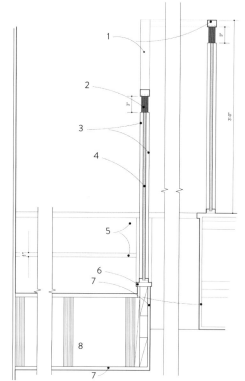

Railing detail at basement stair
Detalle de la barandilla en la escalera del sótano

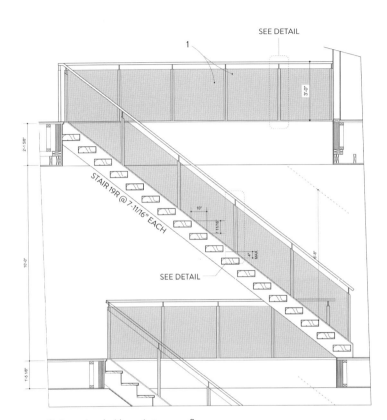

SEE DETAIL

STAIR 19R @ 7-11/16" EACH

SEE DETAIL

Stair section. Inside, main to upper floor
Sección de la escalera. Interior, de la planta principal, al piso superior

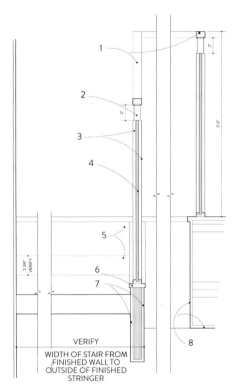

VERIFY
WIDTH OF STAIR FROM
FINISHED WALL TO
OUTSIDE OF FINISHED
STRINGER

Railing detail at stair to upper floor
Detalle de la barandilla de la escalera al piso superior

1. Hardwood handrail
2. Painted steel
3. Hardwood jamb and stop
4. Tempered clear glass
5. Hardwood tread and riser
6. Hardwood cap
7. 1/2" painted MDF
8. 1/2" gypboard

1. Pasamanos de madera
2. Acero pintado
3. Quicio y tope de puerta de madera
4. Vidrio templado transparente
5. Huella y contrahuella de los escalones, de madera
6. Acabado del suelo
7. Tablero MDF (Medium Density Fibreboard) 1/2"
8. Pladur1/2"

Casa Liray

Rubén Rivera Peede
Santiago, Chile
Photos © Rubén Rivera Peede
Area: 115 m²

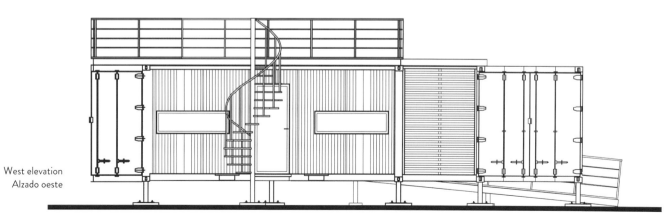

West elevation
Alzado oeste

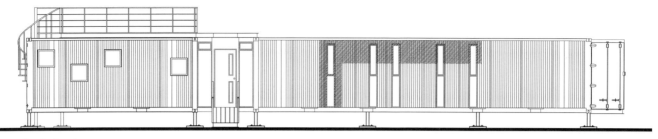

South elevation
Alzado sur

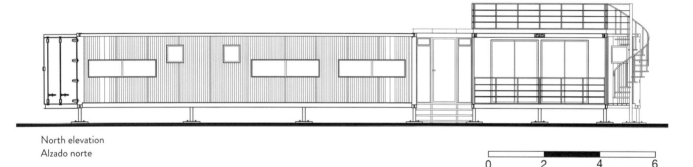

North elevation
Alzado norte

0   2   4   6

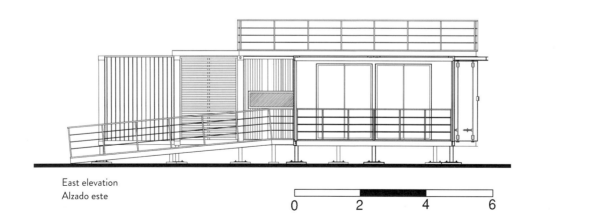

East elevation
Alzado este

0   2   4   6

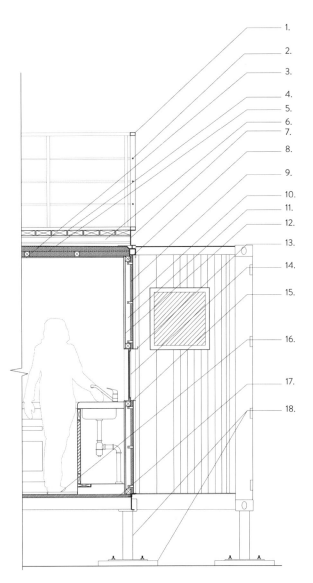

1. Rectangular profile railing 50 x 30 x 2 mm.
2. Clump Ø 12 mm.
3. Gypsum board 10 mm.
4. Impregnated pine table 2 x 6".
5. Projected cellulose insulation.
6. Boardwalk outline 80 x 40 x 15 x 2 mm.
7. Gutter outline 150 x 50 x 2 mm.
8. Upper girder 2 x 2".
9. Projected cellulose insulation.
10. Frange slip of 2 mm.
11. Lintel end 2 x 2".
12. Gypsum board 15 mm.
13. Raincap angle 25 x 25 x 3 mm.
14. Top-hung butt-hinged window.
15. Windowframe plate 50 x 3 mm.
16. Pottery 30 x 30 cm.
17. Original container shuttering.
18. Piling and founding according to calculations.

1. Barandilla de perfil rectangular 50 x 30 x 2 mm.
2. Maciso Ø 12 mm.
3. Placa de yeso cartón 10 mm.
4. Tabla pino impregnado 2 x 6".
5. Aislante de celulosa proyectada.
6. Perfil costanera 80 x 40 x 15 x 2 mm.
7. Perfil canal 150 x 50 x 2 mm.
8. Solera superior 2 x 2".
9. Aislante de celulosa proyectada.
10. Pletina de amarre de 2 mm.
11. Punta de dintel 2 x 2".
12. Placa de yeso cartón de 15 mm.
13. Ángulo cortagotera 25 x 25 x 3 mm.
14. Ventana de aluminio proyectante.
15. Pletina de enmarcación 50 x 3 mm.
16. Cerámica 30 x 30 cm.
17. Placa contrachapada original del contenedor.
18. Pilote y cimentación según cálculos.

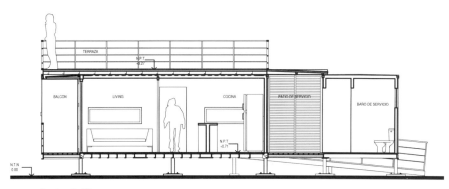

Section B-B'
Sección B-B'

Floor plan
Planta

Section A-A'
Sección A-A'

Pop-Up House

Pop-Up House
Aix-en-Provence, France
Photos © Pop-Up House

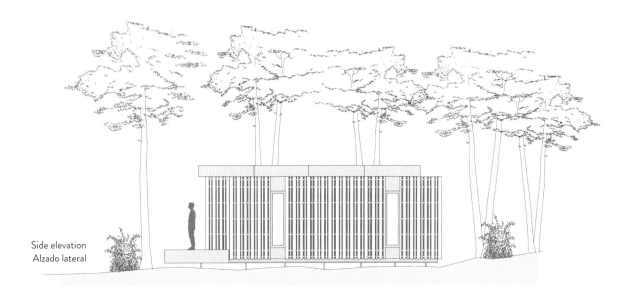

Side elevation
Alzado lateral

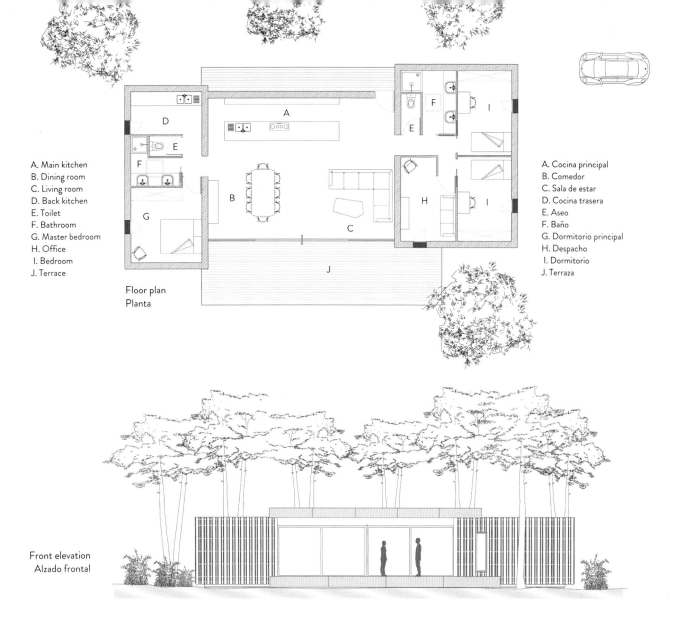

A. Main kitchen
B. Dining room
C. Living room
D. Back kitchen
E. Toilet
F. Bathroom
G. Master bedroom
H. Office
I. Bedroom
J. Terrace

Floor plan
Planta

A. Cocina principal
B. Comedor
C. Sala de estar
D. Cocina trasera
E. Aseo
F. Baño
G. Dormitorio principal
H. Despacho
I. Dormitorio
J. Terraza

Front elevation
Alzado frontal

CONTAINER

New Jerusalem Children's Home

4D and A architects
President Park (Midrand), South Africa
Photos © Denis Guichard
Number of Containers: 28

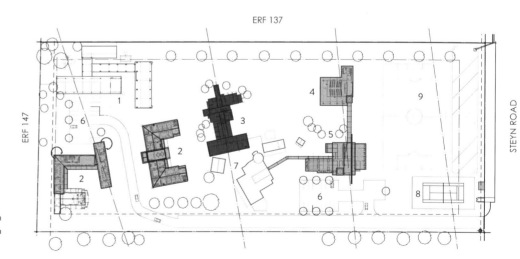

Site plan
Plano de situación

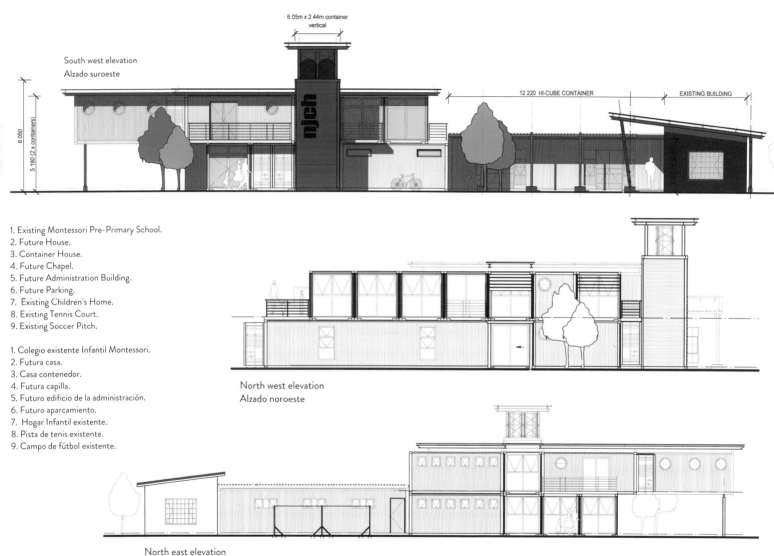

South west elevation
Alzado suroeste

6.05m x 2.44m container vertical

6 050

5 180 (2 x containers)

njch

12 220 HI-CUBE CONTAINER

EXISTING BUILDING

1. Existing Montessori Pre-Primary School.
2. Future House.
3. Container House.
4. Future Chapel.
5. Future Administration Building.
6. Future Parking.
7. Existing Children's Home.
8. Existing Tennis Court.
9. Existing Soccer Pitch.

1. Colegio existente Infantil Montessori.
2. Futura casa.
3. Casa contenedor.
4. Futura capilla.
5. Futuro edificio de la administración.
6. Futuro aparcamiento.
7. Hogar Infantil existente.
8. Pista de tenis existente.
9. Campo de fútbol existente.

North west elevation
Alzado noroeste

North east elevation
Alzado noreste

1. Scullery.
2. Kitchen.
3. Communal dining room.
4. Communal lounge.
5. Children's bedroom.
6. Housemothers unit.
7. Communal homework area.
8. Main entrance lobby.
9. Communal bathrooms.
10. Covered patio.
11. Garden.
12. Washing yard.
13. Staircase.
17. Plant room.

1. Trascocina.
2. Cocina.
3. Comedor comunitario.
4. Salón comunitario.
5. Dormitorio de los niños.
6. Unidad de amas de casa.
7. Área de trabajos comunitarios.
8. Entrada al lobby principal.
9. Baños comunitarios.
10. Patio cubierto.
11. Jardín.
12. Lavandería.
13. Escalera.
17. Habitación.

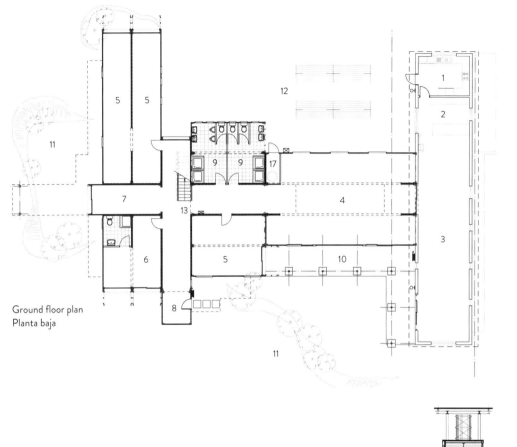

Ground floor plan
Planta baja

2. Kitchen.
4. Communal lounge.
7. Communal homework area.
11. Garden.
12. Washing yard.
13. Staircase.
16. Double volume.

2. Cocina.
4. Salón comunitario.
7. Área de trabajos comunitarios.
11. Jardín.
12. Lavandería.
13. Escalera.
16. Volumen doble.

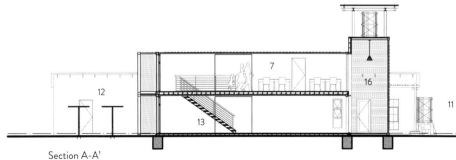

Section A-A'
Sección A-A'

5. Children's bedroom.
6. Housemothers unit.
7. Communal homework area.
9. Communal bathrooms.
13. Staircase.
14. Roof garden.
15. Balcony.
16. Double volume.

5. Dormitorio de los niños.
6. Unidad de amas de casa.
7. Área de trabajos comunitarios.
9. Baños comunitarios.
13. Escalera.
14. Jardín de la azotea.
15. Balcón.
16. Volumen doble.

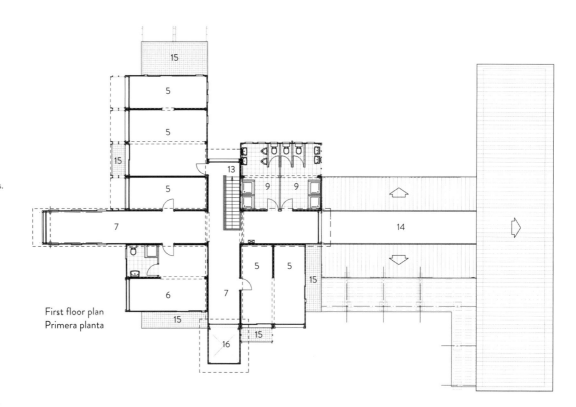

First floor plan
Primera planta

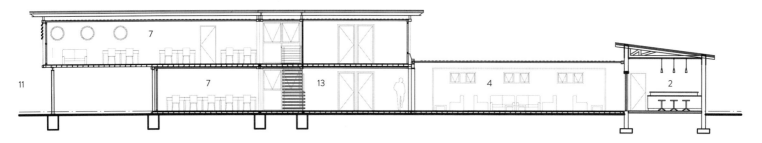

Section B-B'
Sección B-B'

Casa Container

José Schreiber
San Francisco (Córdoba), Argentina
Photos © Arq. Ramiro Sosa
Area: 195 m²

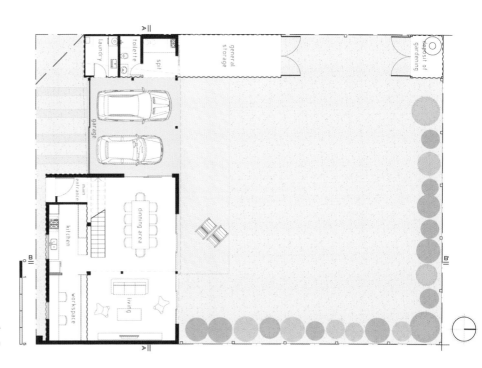

Ground floor
Planta baja

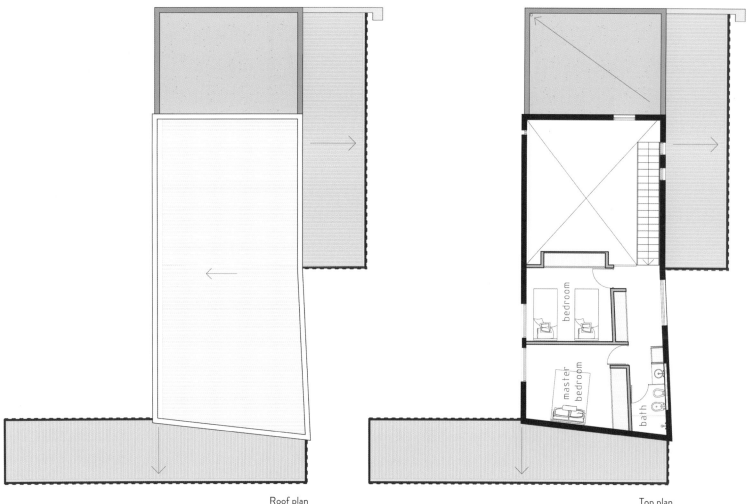

Roof plan
Planta cubierta

Top plan
Planta superior

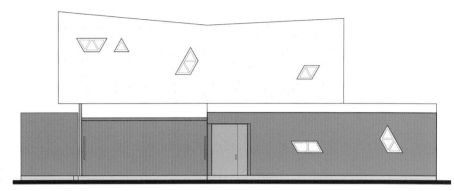

South facade
Fachada sur

North facade
Fachada norte

1. Adquisición de 2 contenedores marítimos.
   Colocación en losas de hormigón.
2. Una unidad está cortada, ajustando las
   dimensiones del lote.
3. El material extraido es usado para el
   portón de los garajes y para espacio de
   almacenamiento.

1. Acquisition of two sea containers. Location on
   concrete slabs.

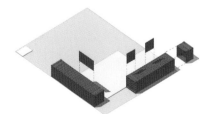

2. One unit is cut, adjusting the dimensions
   of the lot.

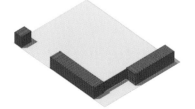

3. The material extracted is used for the gate
   of garages and storage space.

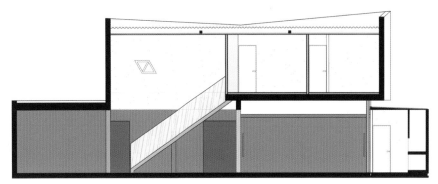

Longitudinal section
Sección longitudinal

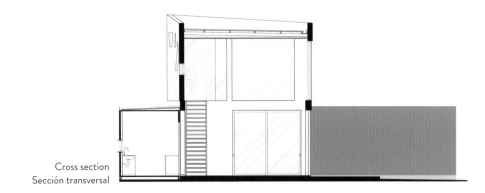

Cross section
Sección transversal

4. Uso de madera de contenedores marítimos
   de la escalera y futuro mobiliario.
5. Columnas, muros y carpintería de aluminio.
   Planta baja abierta (área social)
6. Bloque blanco suspendido sobre los
   contenedores (área privada)

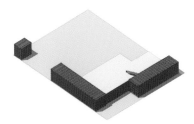

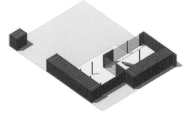

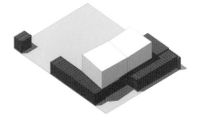

4. Usage of the wood of maritime containers from
   the stair and future furnitures.

5. Columns, walls and aluminium carpentry.
   Open ground floor (social sector)

6. White block floating over the containers
   (private sector)

Kithaus K4

kitHAUS
Brentwood (California), USA
Photos © kitHAUS
Area: 17 m²

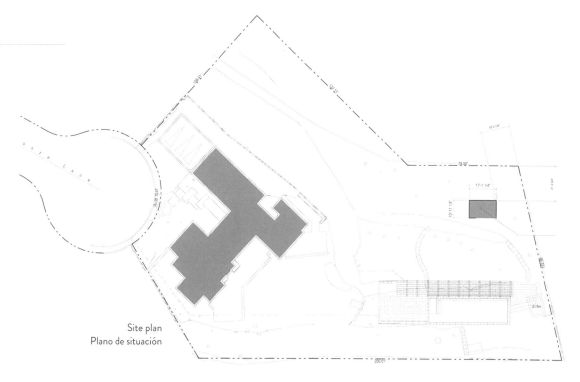

Site plan
Plano de situación

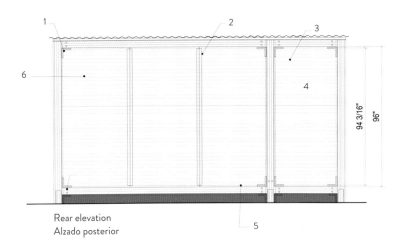

Rear elevation
Alzado posterior

94 3/16"
96"

1. 0-20 Corner brace
2. 4-20 4 x 4 nailer
3. SIP
4. Attach SIP to 4 x 4 at 6" o.c.
5. 6-00 waterproofing under exterior finish.
   Attach to face of extrusion at top, sides and bottom
6. (3) sheets 24 Ga. Corrugated Galvalume® exterior wall finish

1. 0-20 Refuerzo de ángulo
2. 4-20 4 x 4 clavadora
3. SIP (Panel Aislante Estructural)
4. Fijación SIP to 4 x 4 at 6" o.c.
5. 6-00 Acabado exterior impermeabilizado.
   Fijado al panel por arriba, los laterales y la base
6. (3) plancha 24 Ga. Ondulada Galvalume® acabado de pared exterior

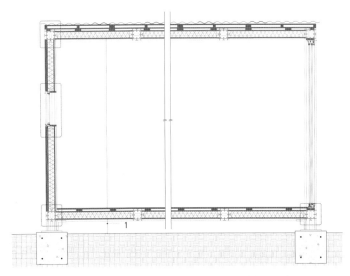

Section
Sección

1. Minimum clearance to grade as required by SIP
   manufacturer 94-1/2" ceiling height
1. La altura mínima requerida por el fabricante es de 94-1/2"

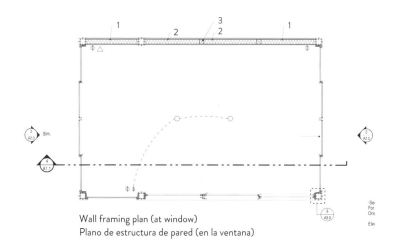

Wall framing plan (at window)
Plano de estructura de pared (en la ventana)

1. 2-03 SIP
2. 2-04 SIP
3 . 4-20 4 x 4 post

1. 2-03 SIP
2. 2-04 SIP
3 . Soporte 4-20 4 x 4

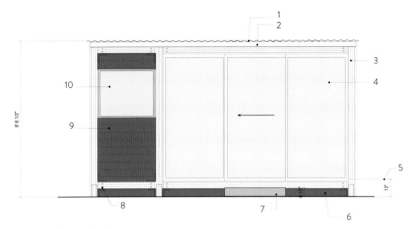

Front elevation
Alzado frontal

1. 24 Ga. Corrugated Galvalume® roofing
2. Galvanized flashing
3. MHS aluminum extrusion (clear anodized)
4. IWC clear anodized aluminum. Framed dual glazed sliding glass door w/low E tempered glass (center panel operable)
5. Finish floor above grade
6. Ipe wood (class A fire rated) 0r 5/16" smooth side cementitious board to enclose under floor area
7. Step by others
8. Bolts facing out
9. 1 x 6 ipe wood exterior wall finish over self-adhesive waterproof membrane
10. IWC Alum. Frame clear anodised dual glazed window with outside temered

1. 24 Ga. Tejado ondulado Galvalume®
2. Tapajuntas galvanizado
3. MHS (Sistema Modular de Construcción de viviendas) aluminio extruido (anodizado)
4. IWC (Innovative Window Concept/Innovador Concepto de Ventana) de aluminio anodizado
5. Suelo acabado en planta baja
6. Madera de nogal (resistencia al fuego clase A) 0r 5/16" tableros lisos cementosos como base aislante
7. Guía de ayuda
8. Tornillos visibles
9. 1 x 6 Pared exterior de madera de nogal fijada sobre una membrana autoadesiva impermeable
10. IWC Alum. Ventana con marco de aluminio anodizado de doble cristal glaseado y el lado externo templado

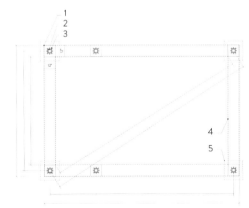

Base plan
Plano de la base

1. Powder coated steel base plate
2. 3 ½" x 3 ½" x ¼" square steel tube
3. MHS aluminum column
4. Grade beam
5. Concrete pad

1. Base de chapa de acero inoxidable tratado con pintura electroestática
2. 3 ½" x 3 ½" x ¼" tubo cuadrado de acero
3. Columna de aluminio MHS
4. Zócalo
5. Losa de hormigón

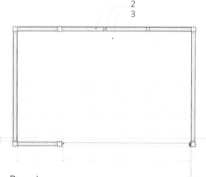

Base plan
Plano de la base

1. Wall SIP
2. 4 x 4 post
3. Palletized ipe wood flooring or approved equal

1. Muro SIP
2. poste 4 x 4
3. Suelo paletizado de madera de nogal o similar aprobado

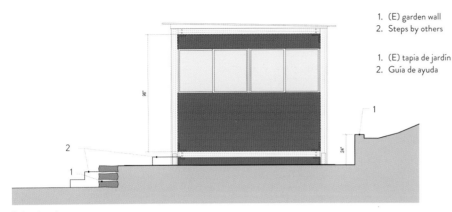

1. (E) garden wall
2. Steps by others

1. (E) tapia de jardín
2. Guía de ayuda

Side elevation
Alzado lateral

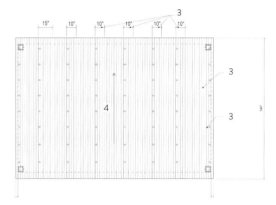

Roof finish plan
Plano de acabado del tejado

1. Overlap of corrugated roof sheets
2. (7) 3-31 sheets class A, 22 Ga. Corrugated Galvalume® roofing
3. Screw locations 18" O.C. at edge + overlap of corrugated sheets. Roof slope 1/2" per 1'-0"

1. Solapamiento de los paneles ondulados del tejado
2. (7) 3-31 Paneles clase A, 22 Ga. Tejado Ondulado Galvalume®
3. Posición de los tornillos 18" O.C. en esquinas + solapamiento de los paneles ondulados. Inclinación del tejado 1/2" por 1'-0"

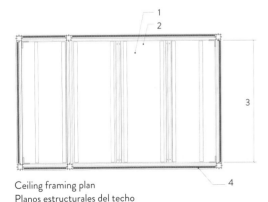

Ceiling framing plan
Planos estructurales del techo

1. 2-01 roof SIP w/ lam. Finish down for interior ceiling finish
2. Roof furring
3. 118" extrusion length
4. Wood filler on top outer channel for roof slope attachment

1. 2-01 techo SIP w/ lam. Acabado interior del tejado
2. Cubierta del tejado
3. 118" longitud extrusionado
4. Masilla para madera en el canal de drenaje del tejado inclinado

Treehouse Riga

Appleton e Domingos Arquitectos
Anywhere
Photos © Fernando Guerra, FG+SG
Area: two 22m^2 modules

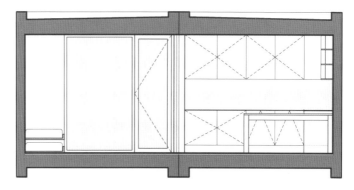

Section B
Sección B

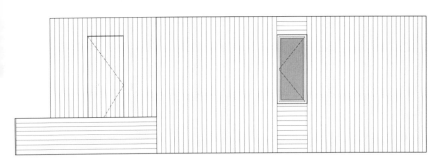

Side elevation
Alzado lateral

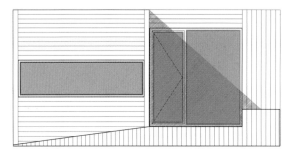

Front elevation
Alzado frontal

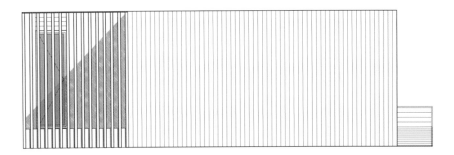

Side elevation
Alzado lateral

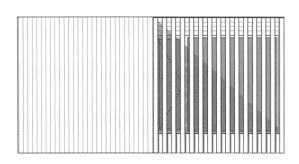

Back elevation
Alzado posterior

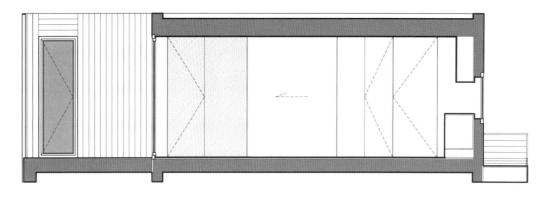

Section A
Sección A

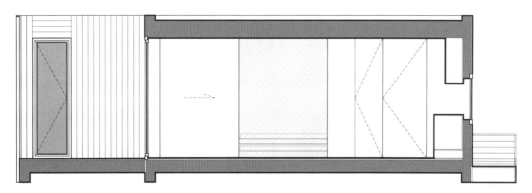

Section A'
Sección A'

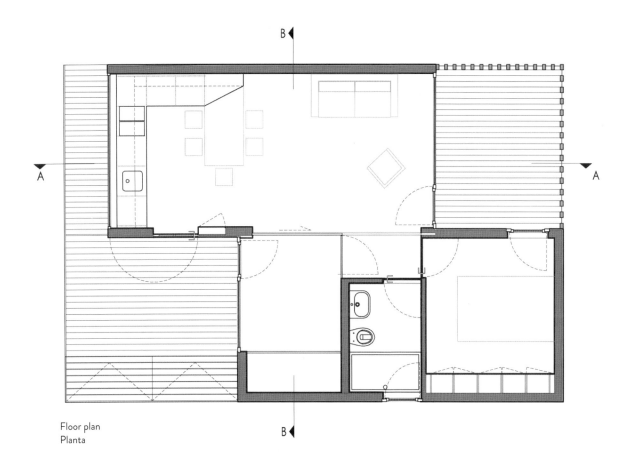

A

B

B

A

Floor plan
Planta

Casa Huiini

S+ diseño. Arq. Sara Tamez
Zapopan (Jalisco), Mexico
Photos © Mito Covarrubias
Area: 148 m^2

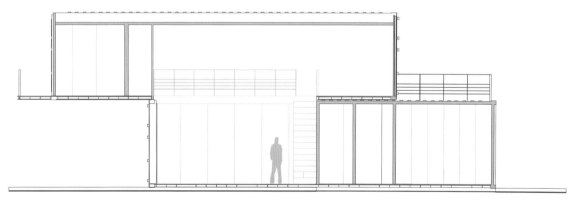

Longitudinal section
Sección longitudinal

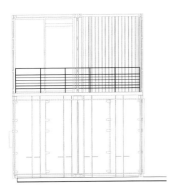

East elevation
Alzado este

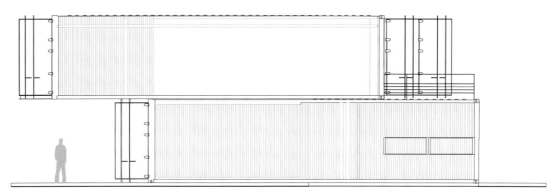

North elevation
Alzado norte

West elevation
Alzado oeste

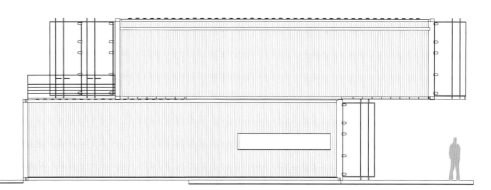

South elevation
Alzado sur

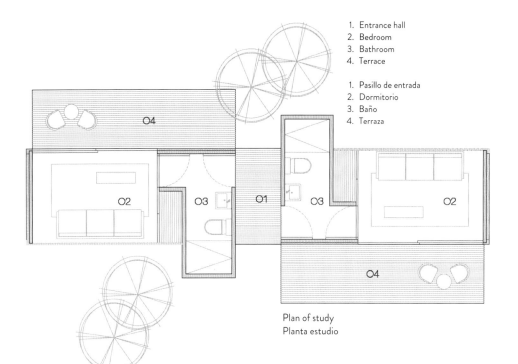

1. Entrance hall
2. Bedroom
3. Bathroom
4. Terrace

1. Pasillo de entrada
2. Dormitorio
3. Baño
4. Terraza

Plan of study
Planta estudio

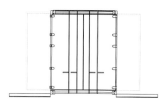

East and west elevation of study
Alzado este y oeste del estudio

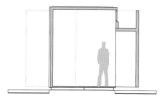

Cross section of study
Sección transversal estudio

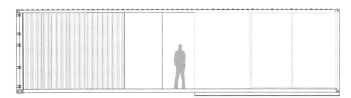

North and south elevation of study
Alzado norte y sur del estudio

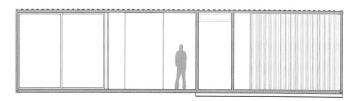

Longitudinal section of study
Sección longitudinal estudio

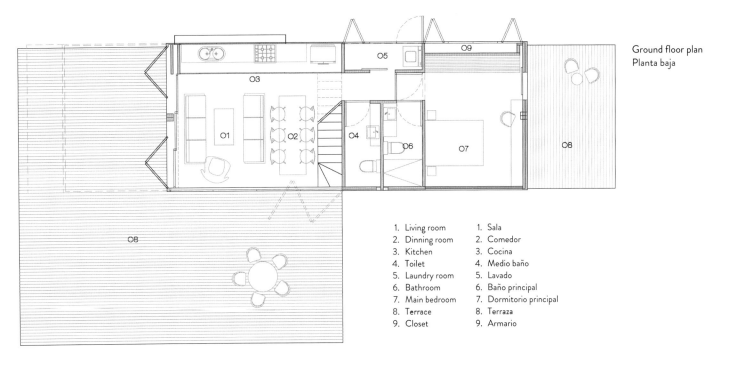

Ground floor plan
Planta baja

1. Living room	1. Sala
2. Dinning room	2. Comedor
3. Kitchen	3. Cocina
4. Toilet	4. Medio baño
5. Laundry room	5. Lavado
6. Bathroom	6. Baño principal
7. Main bedroom	7. Dormitorio principal
8. Terrace	8. Terraza
9. Closet	9. Armario

10. Guest bedroom
11. Guest bathroom and dressing
12. Terrace
13. Hall-Gallery
14. Study

10. Dormitorio visitas
11. Baño y vestidor visitas
12. Terraza
13. Pasillo-Galería
14. Estudio

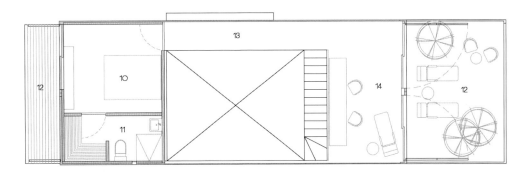

Top floor
Planta superior

Casa en Los Gigantes

Mariana Palacios
Pampa de Pocho (Córdoba), Argentina
Photos © Arq. Gonzalo Viramonte
Living surface: 197 m²
Surface area of garage and warehouse: 52 m²

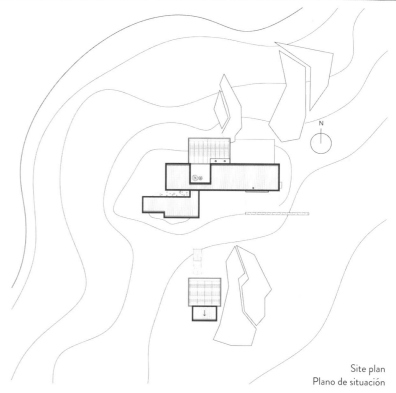

N

Site plan
Plano de situación

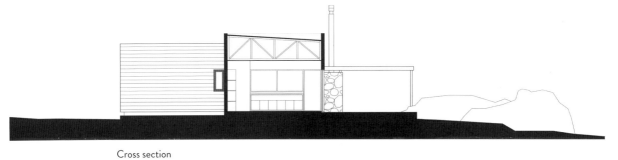

Cross section
Sección transversal

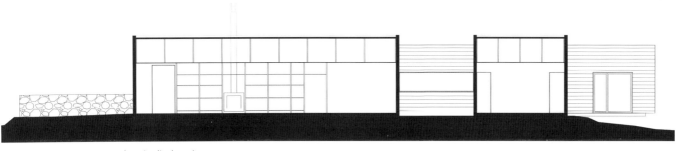

Longitudinal section
Sección longitudinal

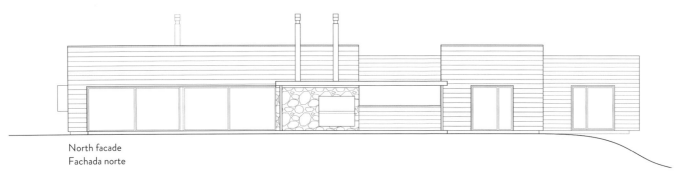

North facade
Fachada norte

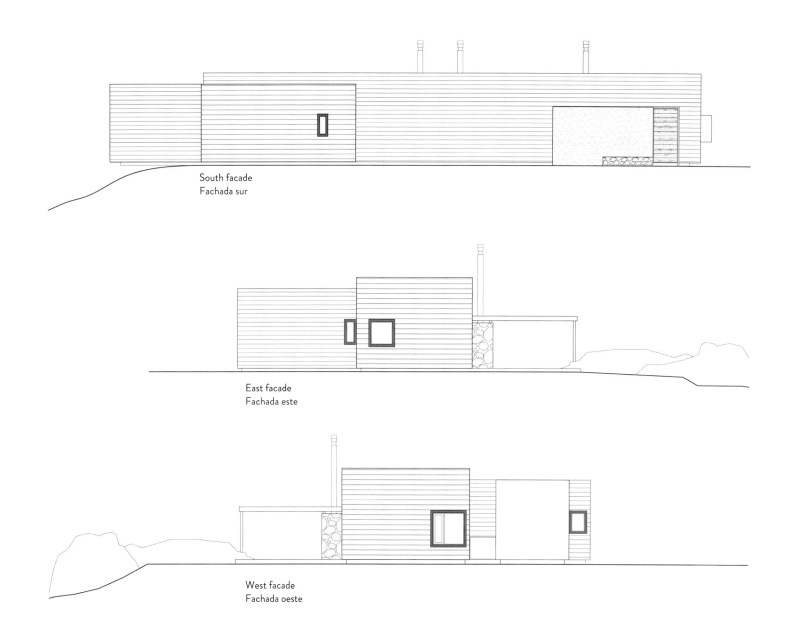

South facade
Fachada sur

East facade
Fachada este

West facade
Fachada oeste

Floor plan
Planta

1. Access
2. Living room
3. Dining room
4. Kitchen
5. Internal courtyard
6. Grill zone
7. Viewpoint terrace
8. Main bedroom
9. Bathroom
10. Friends bedroom
11. Children bedroom
12. Bathroom
13. Restroom
14. Cactus courtyard
15. Garage
16. Tank

1. Acceso
2. Sala de estar
3. Comedor
4. Cocina
5. Patio interno
6. Zona asador
7. Terraza mirador
8. Dormitorio principal
9. Baño
10. Dormitorio invitados
11. Dormitorio niños
12. Baño
13. Antebaño
14. Patio del cactus
15. Cochera
16. Depósito

Camelia Cottage

4site
Melbourne, Australia
Photos © Kevin Hui

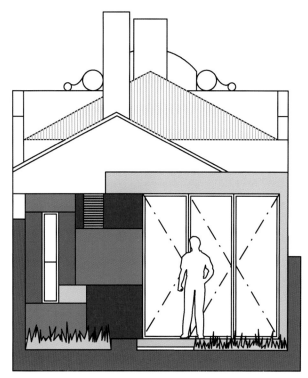

Section D2
Sección D2

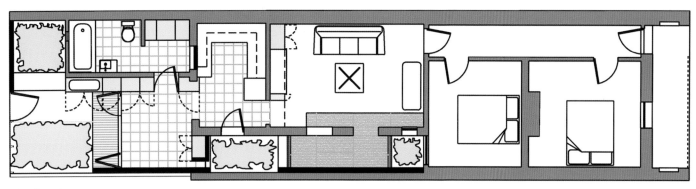

Main floor plan
Planta general

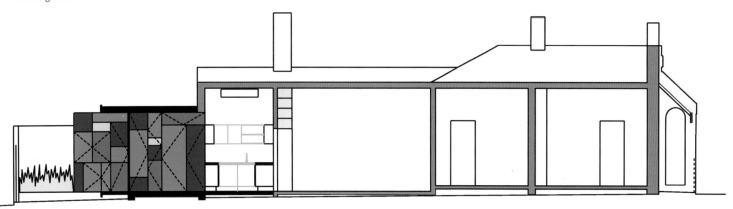

Longitudinal section
Sección longitudinal

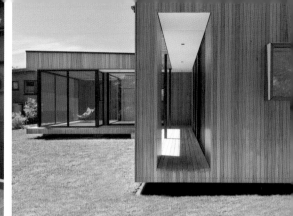

Sorrento House

Archiblox
Sorrento (Victoria), Australia
Photos © Tom Ross | Brilliant Creek

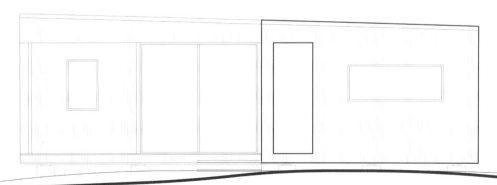

West elevation
Alzado oeste

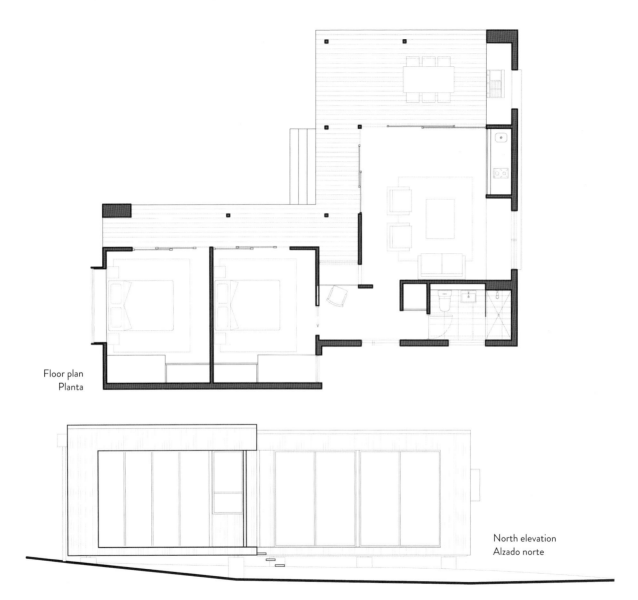

Floor plan
Planta

North elevation
Alzado norte

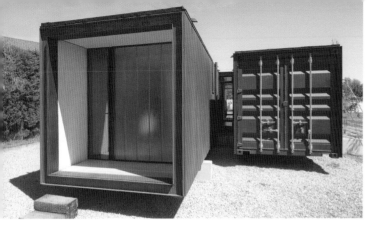

Casa Container 1

Sebastián Irarrázaval Delpiano
Chicureo (Santiago de Chile), Chile
Photos: © Cristóbal Palma
Area: 93 m^2
Number of Containers: 4

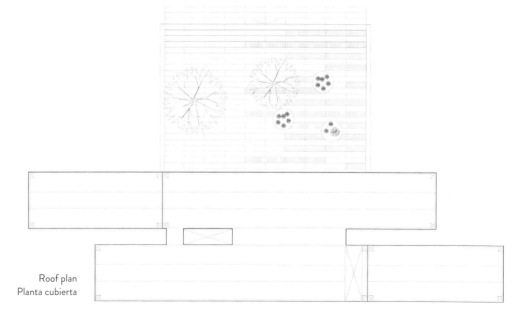

Roof plan
Planta cubierta

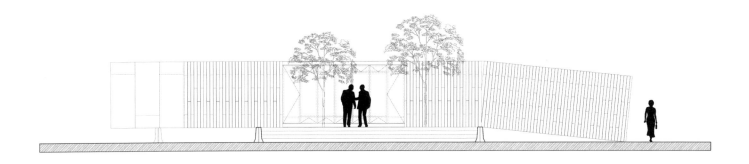

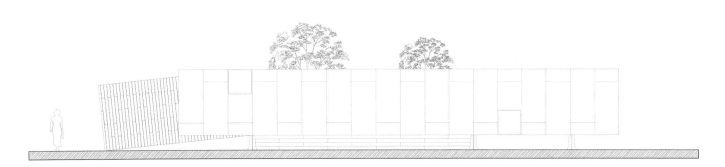

Elevations
Alzados

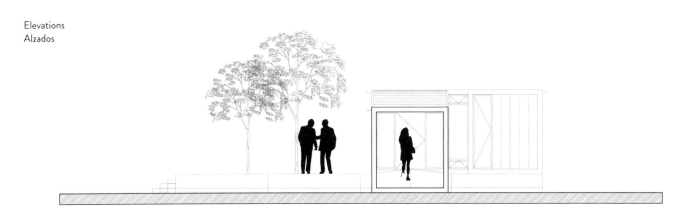

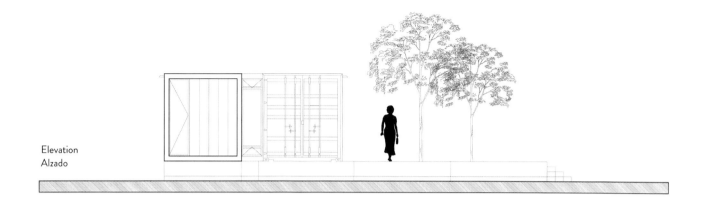

Elevation
Alzado

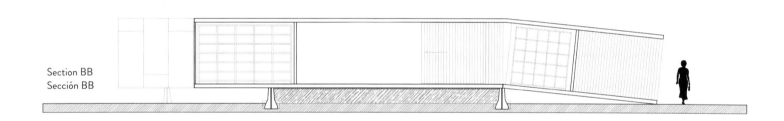

Section BB
Sección BB

Section AA
Sección AA

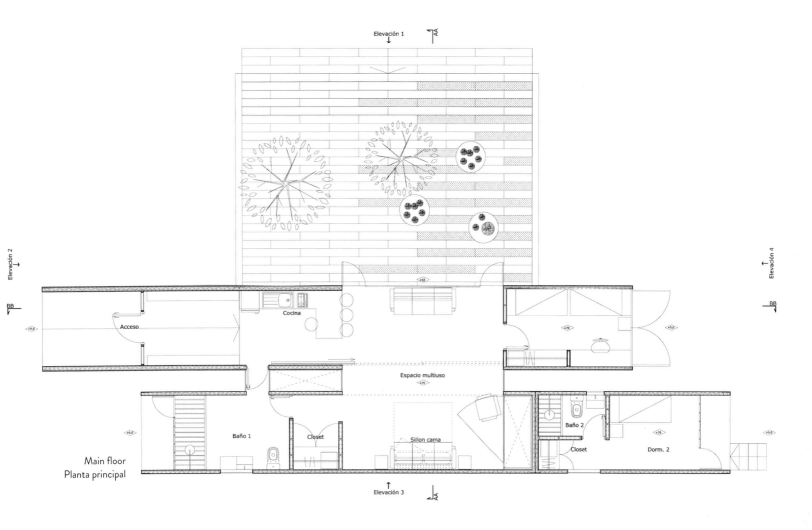

Elevación 1

Elevación 2

Elevación 4

BB

BB

Acceso

Cocina

Espacio multiuso

Baño 1

Closet

Sillon cama

Baño 2

Closet

Dorm. 2

Main floor
Planta principal

Elevación 3

M1 House

Passion Smart Design Houses
Anywhere
Photos © Passion Smart Design Houses

Back elevation
Alzado posterior

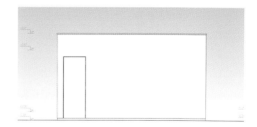

Side elevation
Alzado lateral

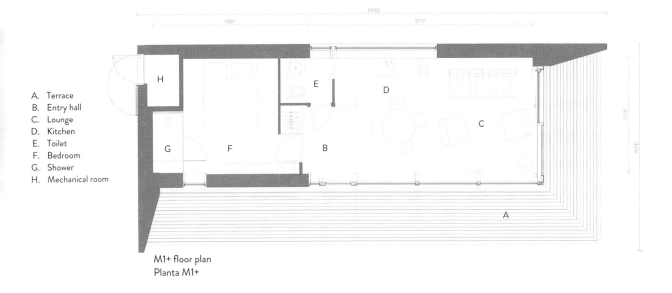

A. Terrace
B. Entry hall
C. Lounge
D. Kitchen
E. Toilet
F. Bedroom
G. Shower
H. Mechanical room

A. Terraza
B. Hall de entrada
C. Salón
D. Cocina
E. Aseo
F. Dormitorio
G. Ducha
H. Sala de máquinas

M1+ floor plan
Planta M1+

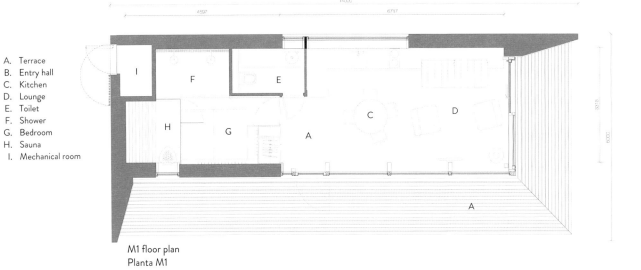

A. Terrace
B. Entry hall
C. Kitchen
D. Lounge
E. Toilet
F. Shower
G. Bedroom
H. Sauna
I. Mechanical room

A. Terraza
B. Hall de entrada
C. Cocina
D. Salón
E. Aseo
F. Ducha
G. Dormitorio
H. Sauna
I. Sala de máquinas

M1 floor plan
Planta M1

1.

ENERGY EFFICIENT
Heating and ventilation
Highly efficient heat ventilation (HRV)
Heat pump for heating and cooling
Electric hot water boiler with sun panel connectivity

2.

COOL
LED lights
All interior and exterior
lights installed

3.

NO WORRIES
Rainwater system
Piping from roof to
rain water drainage

4.

NORDIC STANDARDS
Roof structure
2 layer SBS
Ventilated cavity
Vapor permeable wind barrier
Min 300 mm mineral wool insulation
Nail plate trusses withstanding snow loads up to 3 kN
Finish – Cross-laminated timber

5.

GROOVY
Multimedia appliances
Pre-installed inside and outside
speakers, receiver, TV, internet
ports

6.

DURABLE
Wall structure
Exterior cladding
Ventilated cavity
Vapor permeable wind barrier
250 mm mineral wool insulation
Timber frame structure

7.

INTELLIGENT
Smart home system
Automated controlling security, heating-
cooling, lights, blinds, audio, Co2, humidity

8.

EASY
Sanitary ware and piping
All sanitary ware and
piping pre-installed

9.

RELAX
Fully furnished
Custom made
design furniture

10.

LOW MAINTENANCE
Windows
Aluminum clad wooden
windows with UV
protection triple glazing
units

11.

LONG LASTING
Terrace
Oiled thermo-
treated wood

12.

STRONG FOUNDATION
Floor structure
Interior finish
Concrete slab with under floor heating
Insulation up to 300 mm – EPS

Basic features diagram
Diagrama de las características básicas

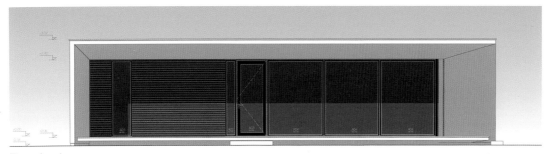

Front elevation
Alzado frontal

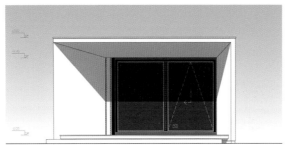

Side elevation
Alzado lateral

1. EFICIENCIA ENERGÉTICA. **Calefacción y ventilación.** Ventilación-calefacción de alta eficiencia (HRV). Bomba de calor para la calefacción y aire acondicionado. Calentador de agua eléctrico con conexión para panel solar.

2. CON ESTILO. **Luces LED.** Todas las luces, exteriores e interiores, instaladas.

3. SIN PREOCUPACIONES. **Sistema de agua de lluvia.** Cañerías desde el tejado al desagüe de agua de lluvia.

4. ESTÁNDARES NÓRDICOS. **Estructura del techo.** 2 capas de SBS. Cavidad ventilada. Paraviento permeable al vapor. Min 300mm de aislamiento de lana natural. Celosías de placa de clavos que soporta cargas de nieve de hasta 3 kN. Acabado – Madera con laminación cruzada.

5. ELEGANTE. **Aplicaciones multimedia.** Altavoces internos y externos, receptor, TV y puertos de internet preinstalados.

6. RESISTENTE. **Estructura de muro.** Exterior enlucido de yeso. Cavidad ventilada. Paraviento permeable al vapor 250mm de aislamiento de lana natural. Estructura de marco de madera.

7. INTELIGENTE. **Sistema de hogar inteligente.** Calefacción-aire acondicionado, luces, persianas, audio, Co2 y humedad controladas automáticamente.

8. FÁCIL. **Sanitarios y cañerías.** Todos los sanitarios y cañerías instalados.

9. RELAX. **Completamente amueblado.** Mobiliario de diseño personalizado.

10. FÁCIL MANTENIMIENTO. **Ventanas.** Ventanas de madera con recubrimiento de aluminio con unidades de acristalado triple para la protección contra rayos UV.

11. DURADERA. **Terraza.** Madera con tratamiento térmico de aceite.

12. CIMIENTOS SÓLIDOS. **Estructura del suelo.** Acabado interior. Losas de hormigón con calefacción bajo el suelo. Aislamiento de hasta 300 mm – EPS

CPH Containers

Tegnestuen Vandkunsten
Location: Copenhagen, Denmark
Photos: © CPH Containers
Total surface: 100 m² (30 inside and 70 outside)

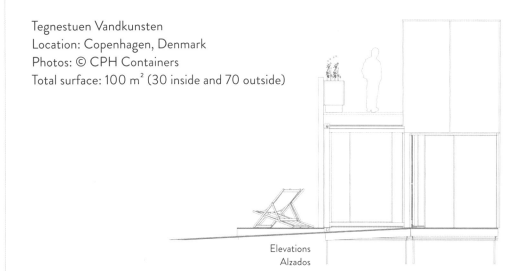
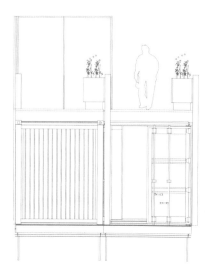

Elevations
Alzados

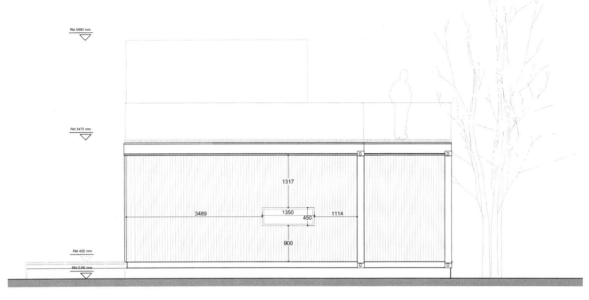

Rkd 5980 mm

Rkd 3475 mm

1317

3489   1350   1114
450

900

Rkd 420 mm
Rkt 0.00 mm

Elevations
Alzados

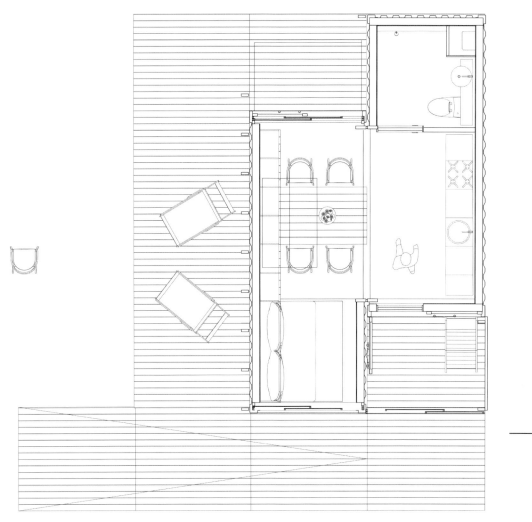

nord

Floor plan
Planta

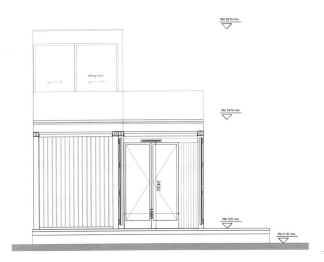

Elevation
Alzado

Section
Sección

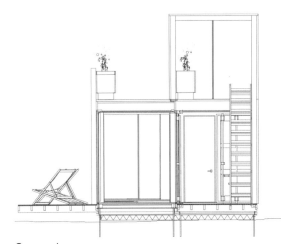

Cross section
Sección transversal

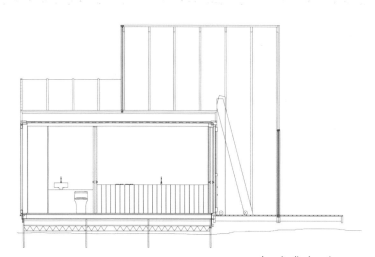

Longitudinal section
Sección longitudinal

Urban Infill 01 & 02

Johnsen Schmaling Architects
Muscoda (Wisconsin), USA
Photos: © John J. Macaulay
Area: 2 units at 85 m² (duplex) or 1 unit at 150 m² (house)

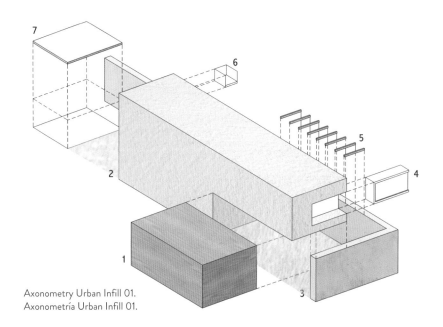

Axonometry Urban Infill 01.
Axonometría Urban Infill 01.

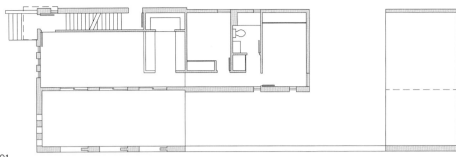

Plans A Urban Infill 01.
Plantas A Urban Infill 01.

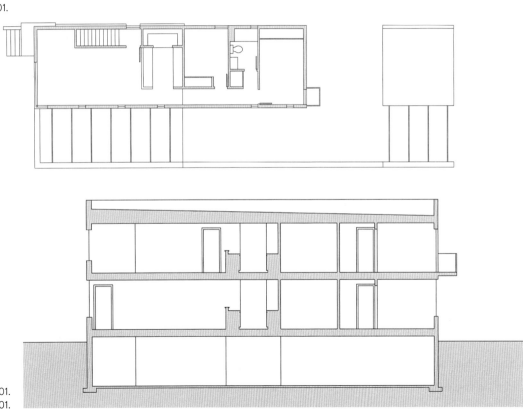

Section A Urban Infill 01.
Sección A Urban Infill 01.

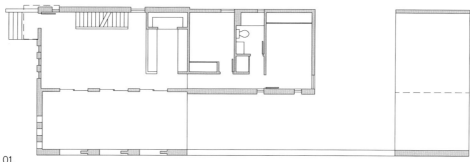

Plans B Urban Infill 01.
Plantas B Urban Infill 01.

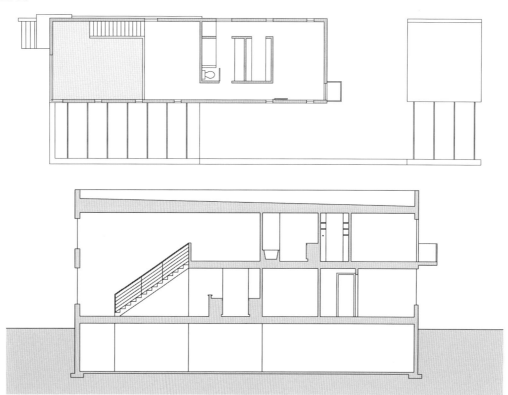

Section B Urban Infill 01.
Sección B Urban Infill 01.

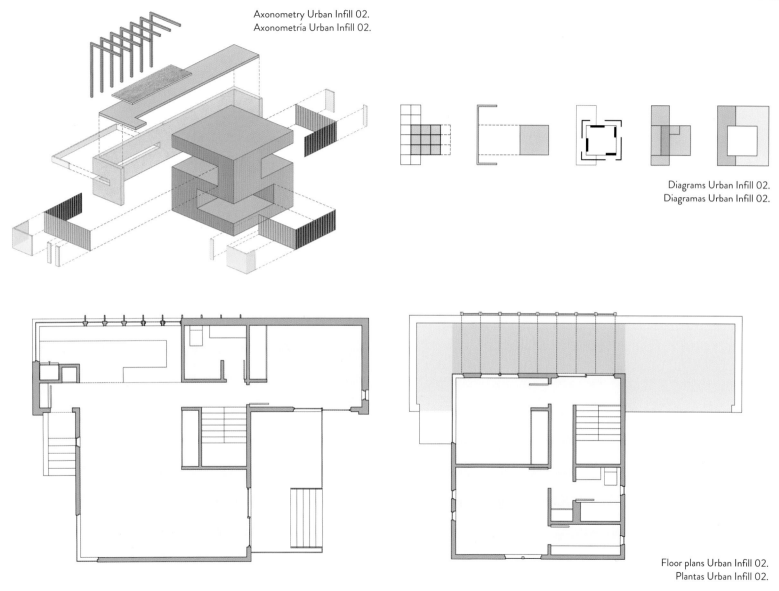

Axonometry Urban Infill 02.
Axonometría Urban Infill 02.

Diagrams Urban Infill 02.
Diagramas Urban Infill 02.

Floor plans Urban Infill 02.
Plantas Urban Infill 02.

Caterpillar House

Sebastián Irarrázaval Delpiano
Lo Barnechea (Santiago de Chile), Chile
Photos © Sebastián Irarrázaval Arquitectos
Area: 350 m²
Number of Containers: 12

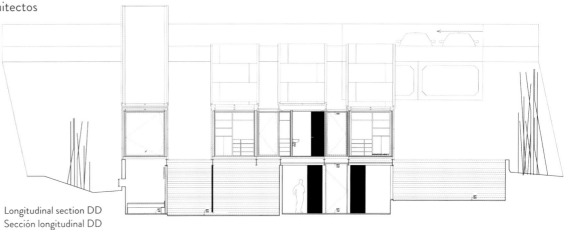

Longitudinal section DD
Sección longitudinal DD

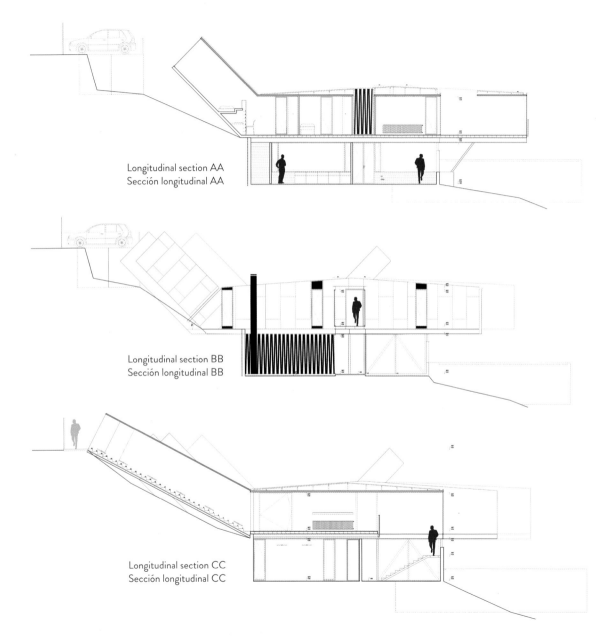

Longitudinal section AA
Sección longitudinal AA

Longitudinal section BB
Sección longitudinal BB

Longitudinal section CC
Sección longitudinal CC

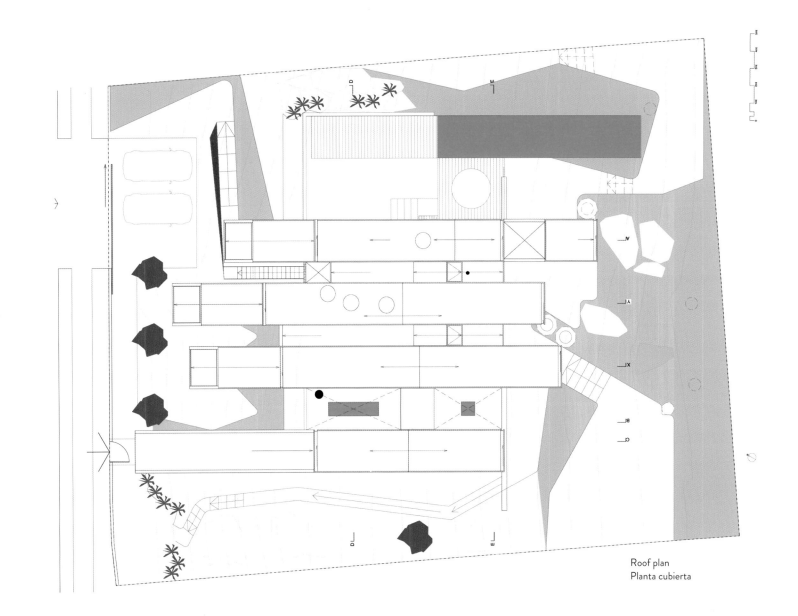

Roof plan
Planta cubierta

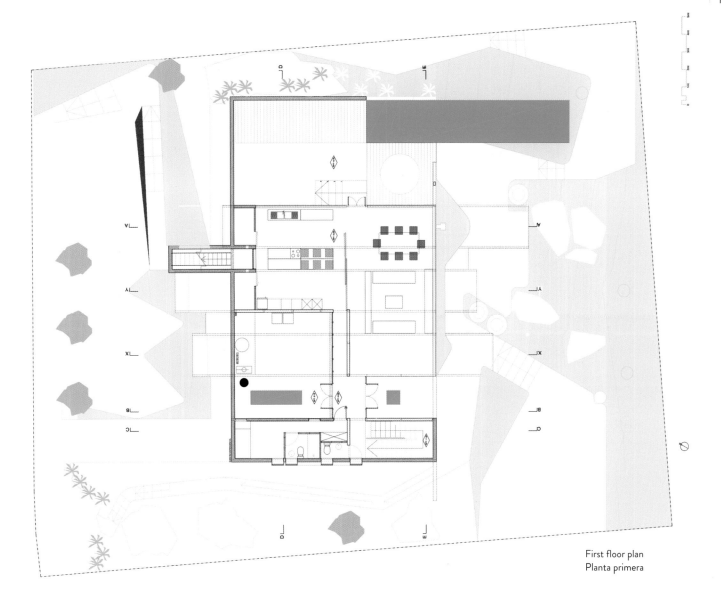

First floor plan
Planta primera

Koby Cottage

Garrison Architects
Albion (Michigan), USA
Photos © Garrison Architects
Area: 102 m²

Section
Sección

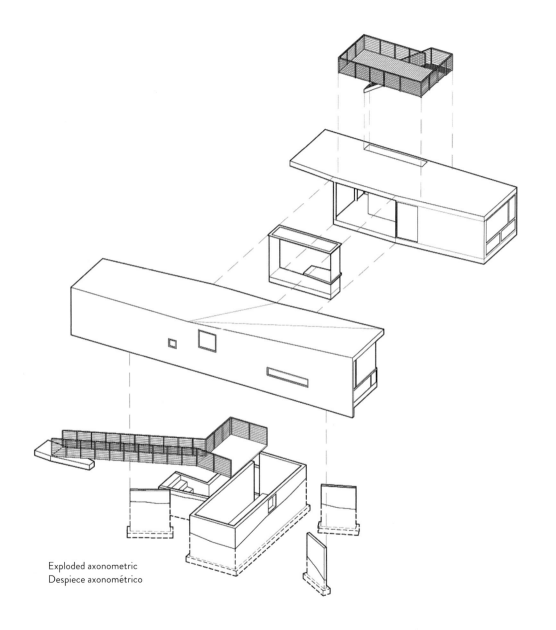

Exploded axonometric
Despiece axonométrico

1. **Heating and cooling**
   High-velocity ducted heating/AC system with heating exchange ventilator
2. **Rainscreen cladding**
   Cor-ten™ steel rainscreen cladding allos to breathe, while resisting water
3. **Banquette/Daybed**
   Banquette with removable bolsters, seats 8, sleeping for 3, upholstered with Climatex® Lifecycle™ fabric
4. **Ceiling and wall finish**
   Tongue & grove FSC-certified pre-finished maple
5. **Flooring**
   Tongue & groove FSC-certified pre-finished maple flooring with 50 years warranty
6. **Fireplace**
   Ecosmart™ non-polluting alcohol burning fireplace
7. **Floor tile**
   Floor-Gres recycled porcelain
8. **Roof integrated photovoltaics**
   Optional thin film photovoltaics
9. **Moisture retardant**
   Smart moisture retardant taped at all seams and openings; breathes in warm weather
10. **Foamed-in-place insulation**
   Foamed-in-place insulation R6.8/inch polyisocyanurate
11. **Continuous insulation**
   Continuous R40/inch Nanopore™ vacuum insulated panel
12. **Steel frame**
   Welded tubular steel frame with high-recycled content
13. **Desk**
   Integrated writing desk
14. **Window system**
   Insulated maple, cedar and stainless steel window system with adjustable neoprene weather stripping
15. **Blinds**
   Integrated roller blinds
16. **High performance glass**
   Heat mirror® Plus R10/UO-10 glazing with low-E coating and argon-filled cavity

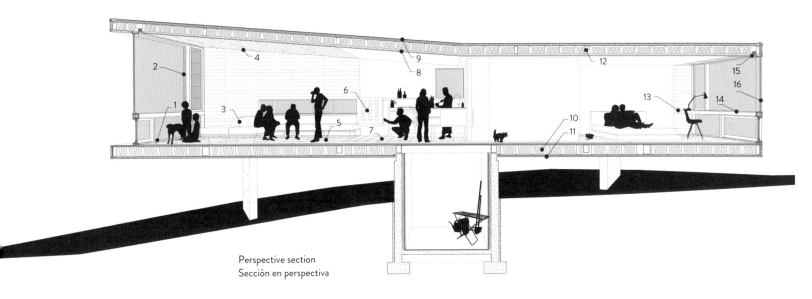

Perspective section
Sección en perspectiva

1. **Calefacción y refrigeración**
   Conductos de calefacción de alta velocidad/Sistema de aire acondicionado con ventilador de intercambio de calor
2. **Fachada ventilada**
   Fachada respirante ventilada de acero Corten™, y resistente al agua
3. **Banqueta / Sofá cama**
   Banqueta con cabezales desmontables, 8 asientos, 3 durmiendo, tapizado en Climatex® Lifecycle™
4. **Acabado de techo y pared**
   Machimembrado en FSC-certificado semi acabado en madera de arce
5. **Suelo**
   Suelo machimembrado en FSC-certificado semi acabado en madera de arce con 50 años de garantía

6. **Chimenea**
   Chimenea Ecosmart™ de alcohol de quemar no polucionante
7. **Suelo de baldosas**
   Suelo de Gres de porcelana reciclado
8. **Techo con paneles solares integrados**
   Fina película fotovoltaica opcional
9. **Retardante de humedad**
   Eficaz retardante de humedad adhesivo en todas las uniones y aberturas al exterior. Respirante con tiempo caluroso.
10. **Aislante de espuma**
    Aislante de espuma R6.8/inch de poliisocianurato
11. **Aislamiento continuo**
    Panel aislante continuo al vacío R40/inch Nanopore™

12. **Estructura de acero**
    Estructura tubular de acero soldado altamente reciclada
13. **Escritorio**
    Mesa escritorio integrada
14. **Sistema de ventanas**
    Ventanas de aislantes de madera de arce, cedro y acero inoxidable con sistema de juntas de neopreno ajustables
15. **Estores**
    Estores integrados
16. **Cristales de alto rendimiento**
    Acristalamiento Heat Mirror® Plus R10/UO-10 de baja emisividad con fina capa de aislante y cámara intermedia rellena de argón

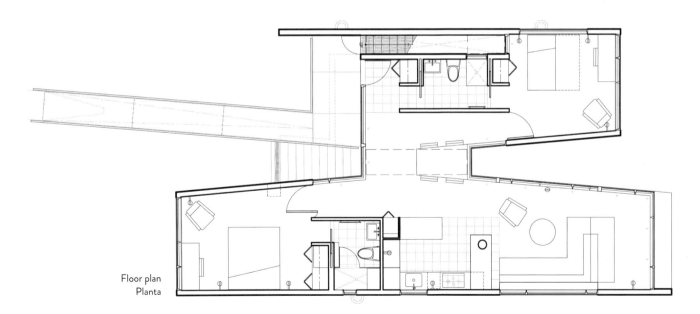

Floor plan
Planta

Modular House

Joaquín Torres & Rafael Llamazares / A-cero
Narón (La Coruña), Spain
Photos © A-cero

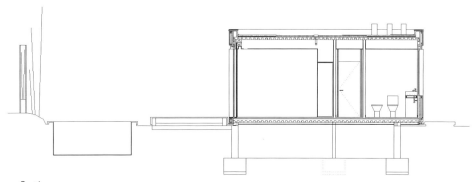

Section
Sección

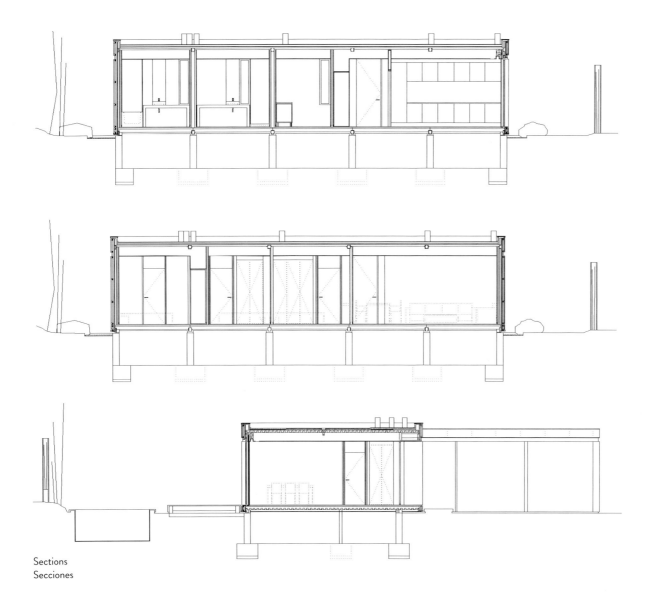

Sections
Secciones

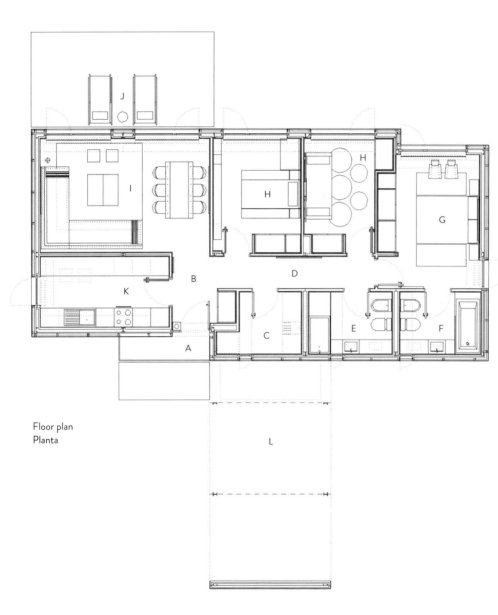

Floor plan
Planta

A. Access
B. Entry hall
C. Laundry room
D. Corridor
E. Bathroom
F. Master bathroom
G. Master bedroom
H. Bedroom
I. Living-dining room
J. Terrace
K. Kitchen
L. Garage

A. Acceso
B. Hall de entrada
C. Cuarto de lavandería
D. Corredor
E. Baño
F. Baño principal
G. Dormitorio principal
H. Dormitorio
I. Salón-Comedor
J. Terraza
K. Cocina
L. Garaje

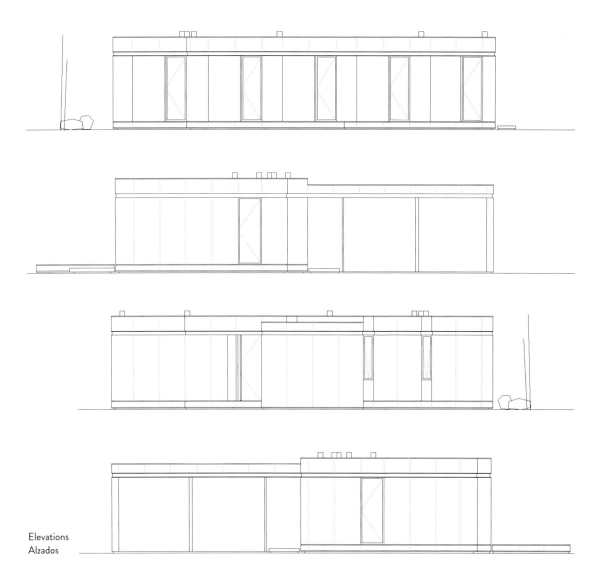

Elevations
Alzados

Casa Incubo

María José Trejos
Escazú (San José), Costa Rica
Photos © Sergio Pucci
Area: 400 m²

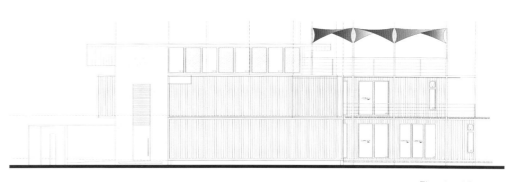

Elevation right
Alzado derecho

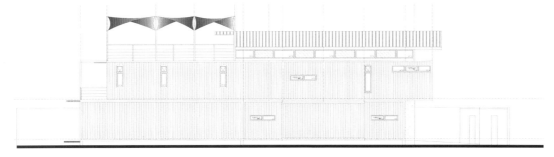

Elevation left
Alzado izquierdo

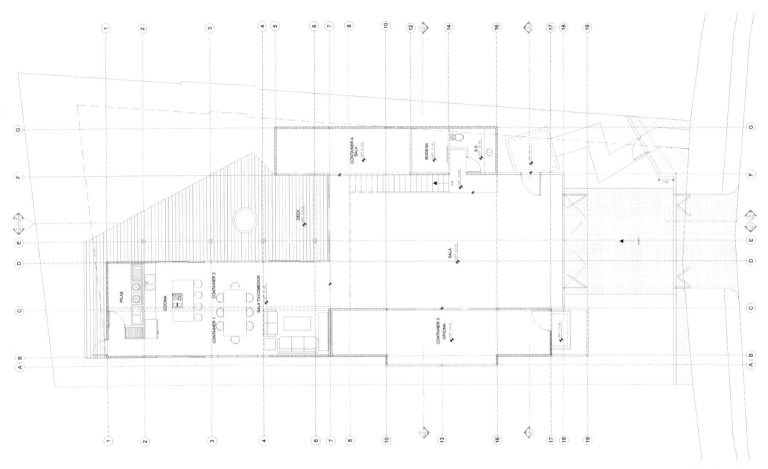

First floor plan
Primer piso

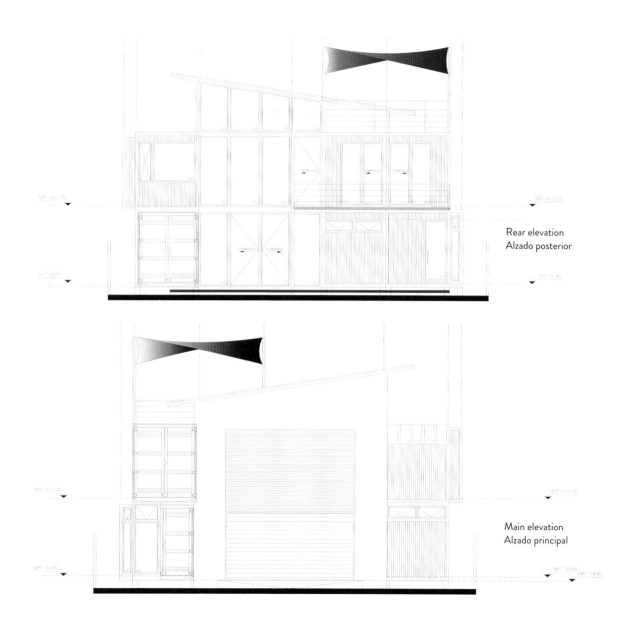

Rear elevation
Alzado posterior

Main elevation
Alzado principal

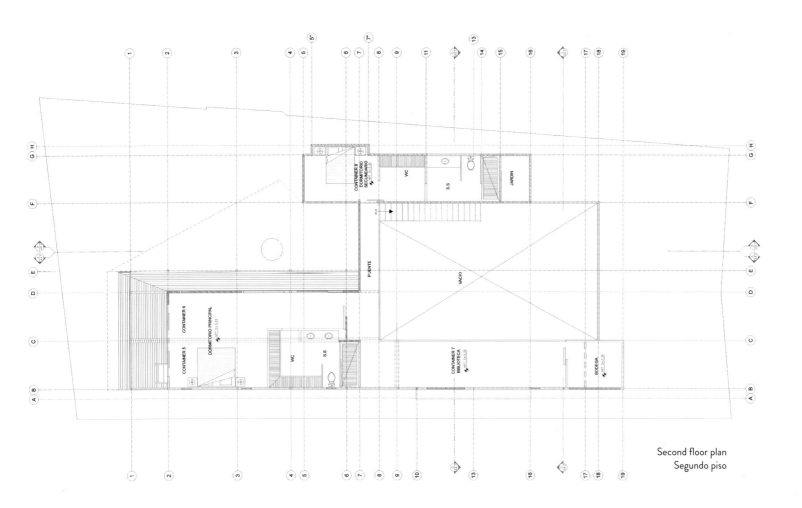

Second floor plan
Segundo piso

Nomad Living Sives

studio arte
Silves, Portugal
Photos © studio arte

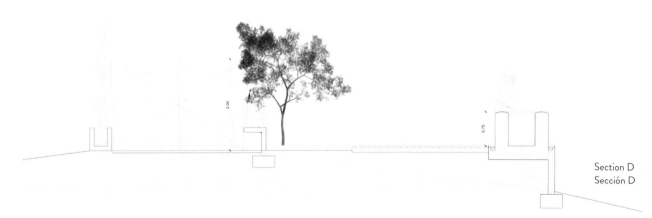

Section D
Sección D

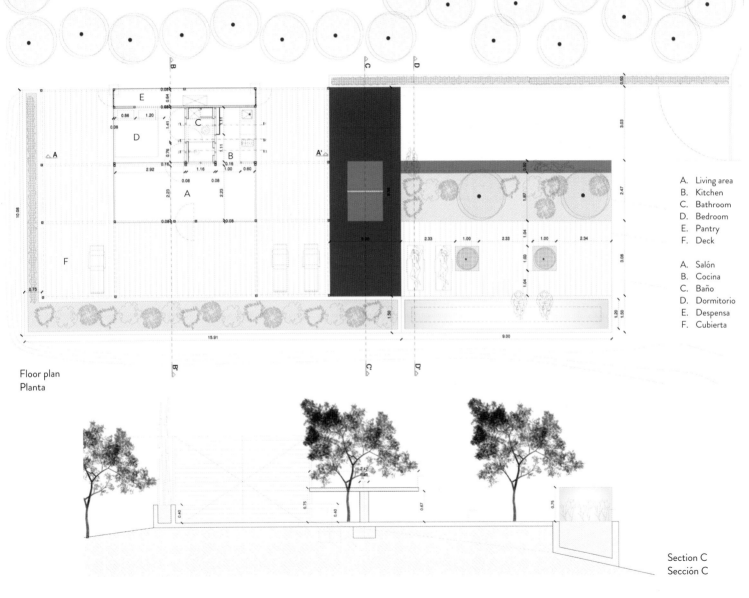

A. Living area
B. Kitchen
C. Bathroom
D. Bedroom
E. Pantry
F. Deck

A. Salón
B. Cocina
C. Baño
D. Dormitorio
E. Despensa
F. Cubierta

Floor plan
Planta

Section C
Sección C

B-Line Medium 003

Hive Modular
Minneapolis (Minnesota), USA
Photos © Hive Modular

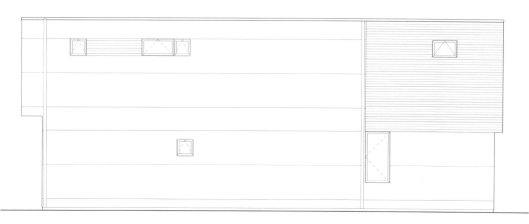

North elevation
Alzado norte

South elevation
Alzado sur

West elevation
Alzado oeste

East elevation
Alzado este

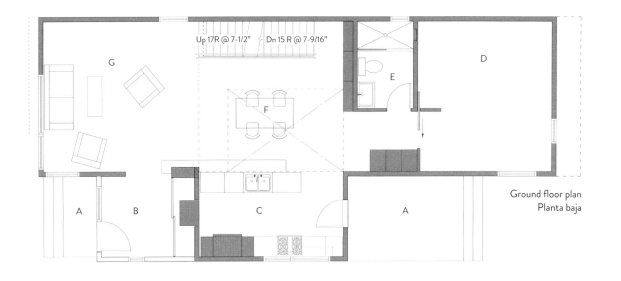

Up 17R @ 7-1/2"   Dn 15 R @ 7-9/16"

G

D

E

F

A   B   C   A

Ground floor plan
Planta baja

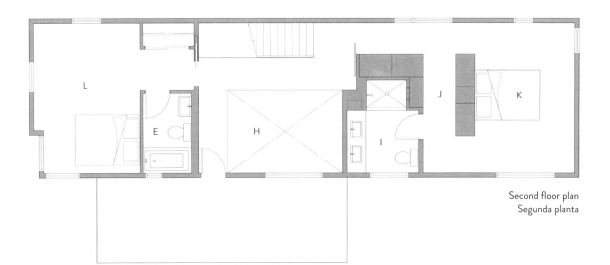

L

E   H   J   K

I

Second floor plan
Segunda planta

A. Deck
B. Entry
C. Kitchen
D. Bedroom
E. Bathroom
F. Dining room
G. Living room
H. Open to below
I. Master bathroom
J. Master closet
K. Master bedroom
L. Bedroom

A. Cubierta
B. Entrada
C. Cocina
D. Dormitorio
E. Baño
F. Comedor
G. Salón
H. Abertura con vista abajo
I. Baño principal
J. Armario
K. Dormitorio principal
L. Dormitorio

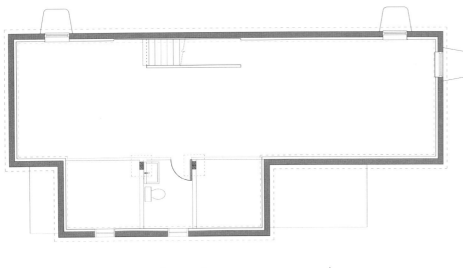

Basement floor plan
Planta sótano

1. Hardwood handrail
2. Welded barstock brackets with holes for handrail attachment and stringer connection
3. C9 x 20 stringer, typ.
4. 2" x 2" angles or sug. for floor pan attachment
5. 2" x 2" angles or sug. welded @ ends to tread pan for attachment
6. 10 GA tread pan bent as shown with 5/4" hardwood stair tread attached from below
7. 5/4" hardwood stair tread
8. Leave 3-1/2" space between stringer and lexan
9. Leave 3-1/2" space between handrail and lexan
10. Screw lexan to spindles w/large banjo washers

1. Pasamanos en madera de ley
2. Soportes de varilla soldado con agujeros para fijar el pasamanos y los escalones a la zanca
3. Tirantes tipo C9 x 20
4. Ángulos para fijación de los paneles del suelo de 2"x 2"
5. Ángulos de 2"x 2" para sujetar el panel del escalón a la fijación
6. Escalón curvado de 10 GA como indicado, de 5/4", de madera de ley sujetado desde abajo
7. Escalón en madera de ley de 5/4"
8. Dejar 3-1/2" de espacio entre zanca y lexan
9. Dejar 3-1/2" de espacio entre pasamanos lexan
10. Atornillar el lexan a los barrotes con una arandela ancha

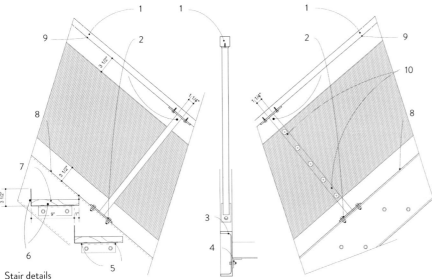

Stair details
Detalles escalera

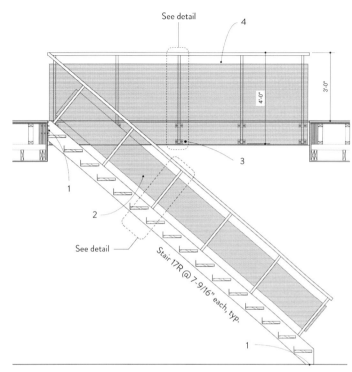

See detail

4

See detail

3'-0"

4'-0"

3

1

2

Stair 17R @ 7-9/16" each, typ.

1

Section view of inside of stair balustrade and outside of walkway guardrail above
Vista de la sección del interior de la balaustrada y del lado exterior de la barandilla desde arriba

1. XField bolt stair to house structure
2. Lexan mechanically fastened to outside of stair rail
3. Field install spindles bolted to floor, typ.
4. Lexan mechanically fastened to outside of walkway rails

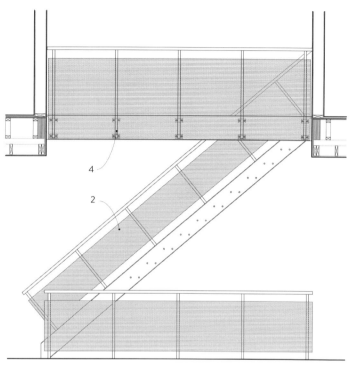

4

2

Section view of outside of stair balustrade and outside of walkway guardrail above
Vista de la sección del exterior de la balaustrada y del lado exterior de la barandilla desde arriba

1. Perno Xfield para la estructura
2. Lexan para fijación exterior barandilla
3. Barrotes atornillados al suelo
4. Lexan fijado mecánicamente al exterior de los rieles de la pasarela

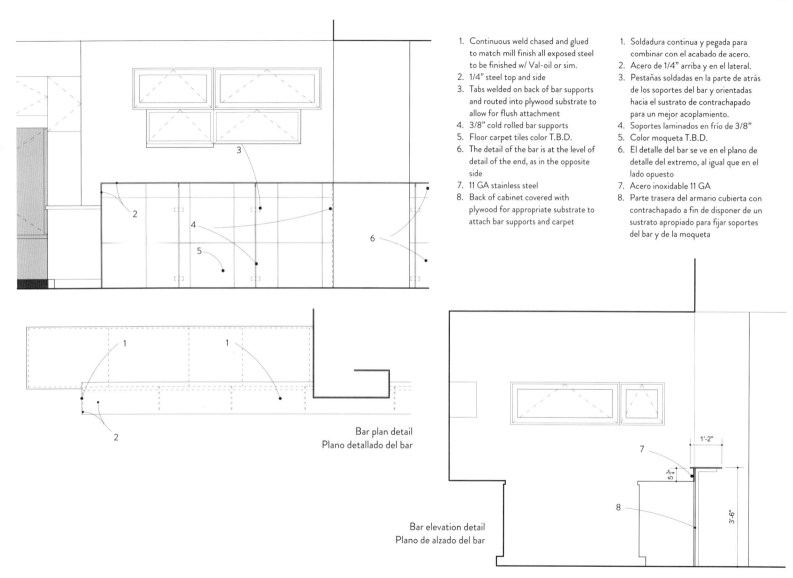

1. Continuous weld chased and glued to match mill finish all exposed steel to be finished w/ Val-oil or sim.
2. 1/4" steel top and side
3. Tabs welded on back of bar supports and routed into plywood substrate to allow for flush attachment
4. 3/8" cold rolled bar supports
5. Floor carpet tiles color T.B.D.
6. The detail of the bar is at the level of detail of the end, as in the opposite side
7. 11 GA stainless steel
8. Back of cabinet covered with plywood for appropriate substrate to attach bar supports and carpet

1. Soldadura continua y pegada para combinar con el acabado de acero.
2. Acero de 1/4" arriba y en el lateral.
3. Pestañas soldadas en la parte de atrás de los soportes del bar y orientadas hacia el sustrato de contrachapado para un mejor acoplamiento.
4. Soportes laminados en frío de 3/8"
5. Color moqueta T.B.D.
6. El detalle del bar se ve en el plano de detalle del extremo, al igual que en el lado opuesto
7. Acero inoxidable 11 GA
8. Parte trasera del armario cubierta con contrachapado a fin de disponer de un sustrato apropiado para fijar soportes del bar y de la moqueta

Bar plan detail
Plano detallado del bar

Bar elevation detail
Plano de alzado del bar

Two-Tree House

Golany Architects
Jerusalem, Israel
Photos © Yaron Golany
Number of Containers: 2

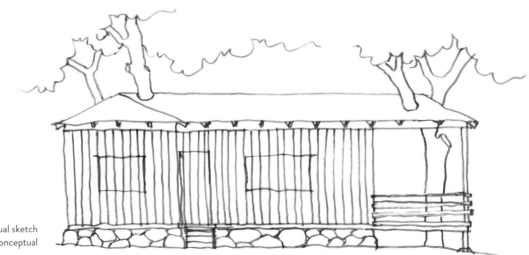

Conceptual sketch
Boceto conceptual

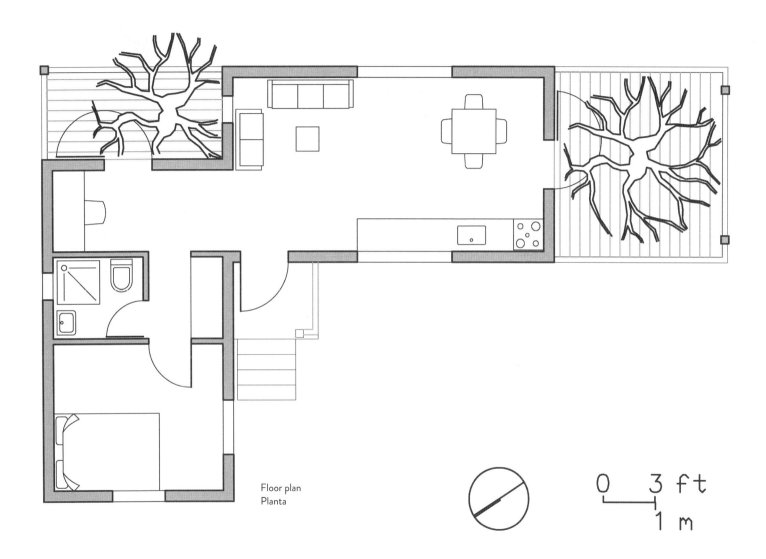

Floor plan
Planta

0   3 ft
1 m

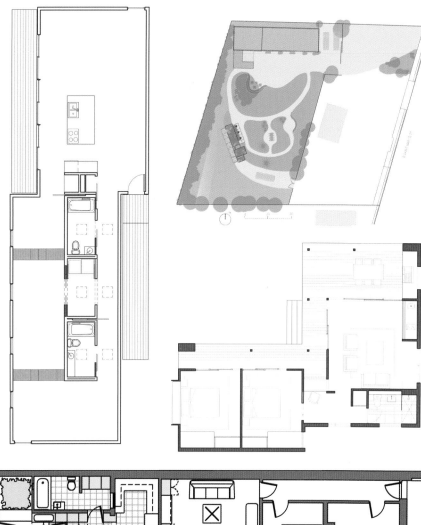
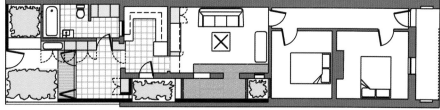